DRAGON BALL Z

STORY & ART BY

AKIRA TORIYAMA

Dragon Ball Z
Volume 1
VIZBIG Edition

STORY AND ART BY
AKIRA TORIYAMA

English Adaptation **Gerard Jones**
Translation **Lillian Olsen**
Touch-up Art & Lettering **Wayne Truman**
Shonen Jump Series Design **Sean Lee**
VIZBIG Edition Design **Courtney Utt**
Shonen Jump Series Editor **Jason Thompson**
VIZBIG Edition Editors **Leyla Aker, Amy Yu**

Printed in China

Published by VIZ Media, LLC
P.O. Box 77010
San Francisco, CA 94107

13
First printing, May 2008
Thirteenth printing, September 2021

www.viz.com

DRAGON BALL Z

VOLUME 1
THE WORLD'S GREATEST TEAM

VOLUME 2
THE LORD OF WORLDS

VOLUME 3
EARTH VS. THE SAIYANS

STORY & ART BY
AKIRA TORIYAMA

SHONEN JUMP MANGA . VIZBIG EDITION

CONTENTS

VOLUME 2
THE LORD OF WORLDS

VOLUME 3
EARTH VS. THE SAIYANS

CAST OF CHARACTERS

Tenshinhan
Three-eyed Tenshinhan is one of Goku's former rivals.
Yamcha
A former bandit and a martial artist, Yamcha is Bulma's ex-boyfriend.
Bulma
A friend who has known Goku longer than anybody. Bulma is a scientific genius who met Goku while on a quest for the seven magical Dragon Balls.
Kuririn
Goku's former martial arts school-mate under Kame-Sen'nin.
Son Goku
The greatest martial artist the world has ever known. Goku can produce the energy blast called the *Kamehameha* and rides a flying cloud called the *Kinto'un*. When he was younger, he used to have a tail like a monkey's. Five years ago, he married Chi-Chi and had a son.
Son Gohan
Goku's 4-year-old son with his wife Chi-Chi.

Kame-Sen'nin
Kame-Sen'nin, also known as the "Turtle Hermit" or *Muten-Rōshi* (the "invincible Old Master"), helped train Goku and Kuririn in the martial arts.
Vegeta & Nappa
The two mighty Saiyan warriors.
Piccolo
Goku's archenemy, Piccolo *Daimaō* ("Piccolo the Great Demon King") once tried to become ruler of the world. The score was settled five years ago when Goku battled Piccolo at the Tenka'ichi Budōkai world fighting tournament.
Kami-sama
The deity who watches over the Earth, Kami-sama is the good side to Piccolo's evil. He is assisted by Mr. Popo.
Chi-Chi
Goku's wife and Gohan's mother, Chi-Chi has a tendency to overreact.
Raditz
This mysterious warrior is one of the most powerful foes Goku has ever encountered.
Kaiō-sama
Also known as the "Lord of Worlds," he is Kami-sama's superior in the heavenly bureaucracy. He lives in the Other World at the end of the Serpent Road.
Chaozu
Tenshinhan's best friend and former schoolmate.

DragonBallZ

VOLUME 1

THE WORLD'S GREATEST TEAM

DBZ: 01 · The Mysterious Warrior from Space

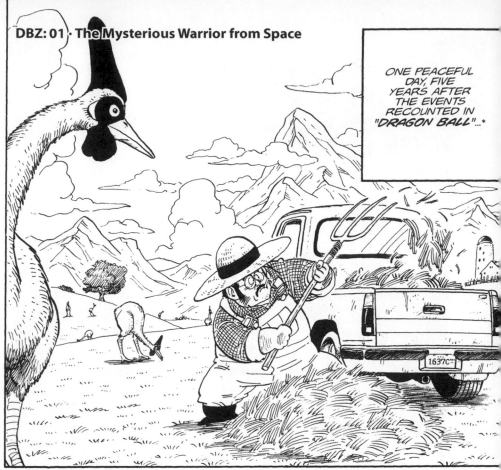

ONE PEACEFUL DAY, FIVE YEARS AFTER THE EVENTS RECOUNTED IN "**DRAGON BALL**"...*

1637C

*AS IN THE OTHER **DRAGON BALL** (WITHOUT THE **Z**) COMIC PUBLISHED BY VIZ, WHICH TELLS THE STORY OF GOKU'S CHILDHOOD.

EEENNNN...
WHA' ?!
WAA !!

I-I-I-IT'S A METEOR!!
OR A UF-F-F-F-O !!

DOOM
EEE-YAAA !!!!

I GOTTA SEE !!
VROOM VROOM...

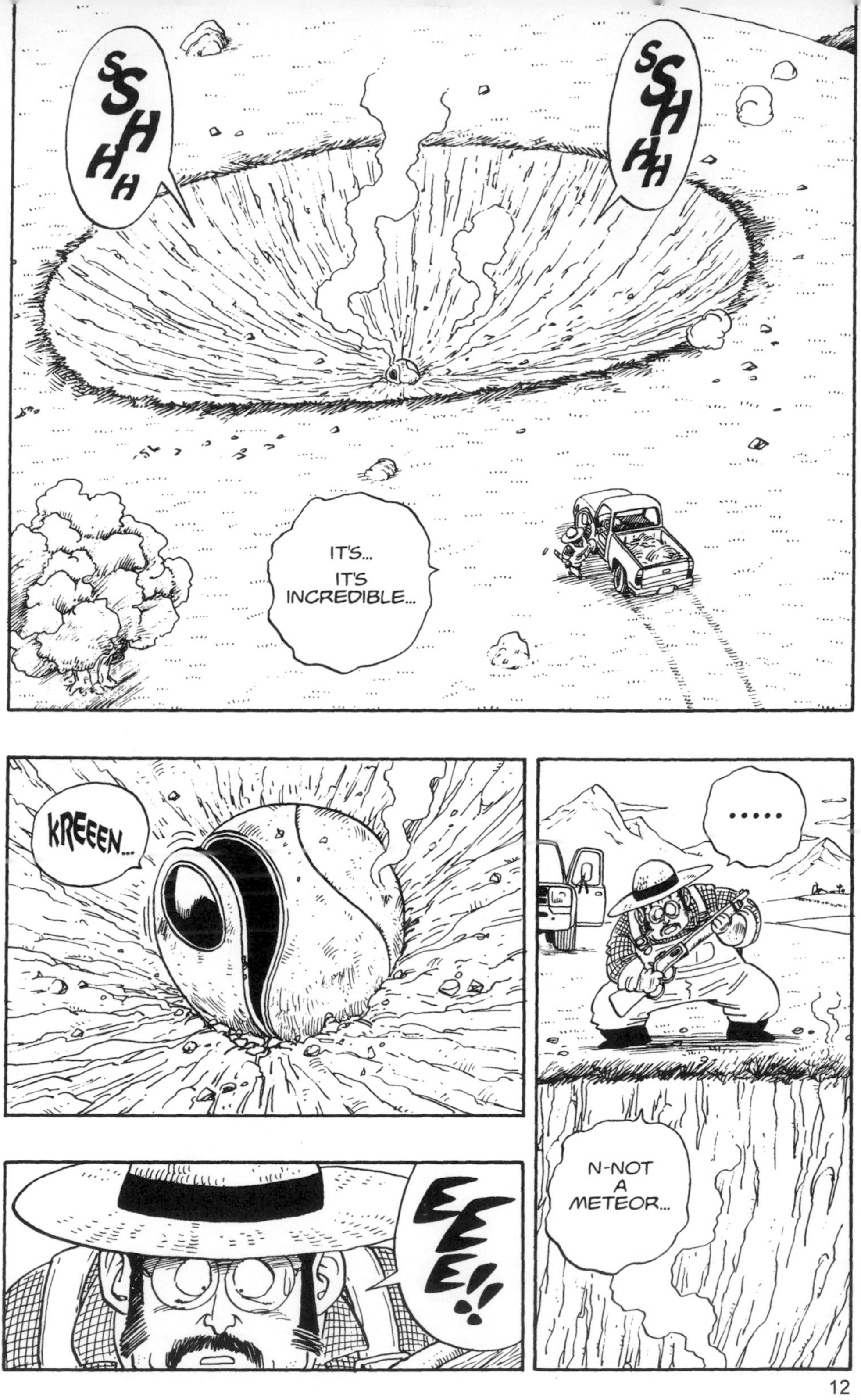

SSHHH

SSHHH

IT'S...
IT'S INCREDIBLE...

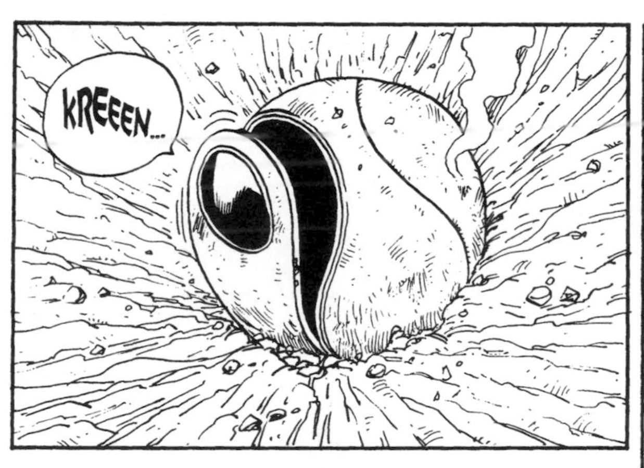

UH...
UHH...

SO...THE INHABITANTS OF THIS WORLD ARE STILL ALIVE...
CURSE THAT *KAKARROT*...

SHMMM
!!

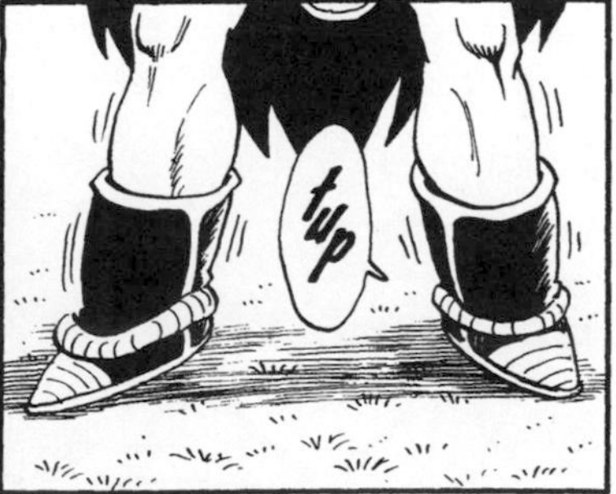
tup

ST-
STOP!!
WHO ARE
YOU?!!!

eep-
eep...
POWER
LEVEL...
ONLY FIVE.
WHAT A
PLANET!

ST-
STAY
AWAY
!!
I'M
WARNING
YOU!

WAAAH!
BOOM

PAP

AAA !!!
NOOO !!!

PIP

PLAP

FEH.
A PLANET OF WEAKLINGS...

eep...

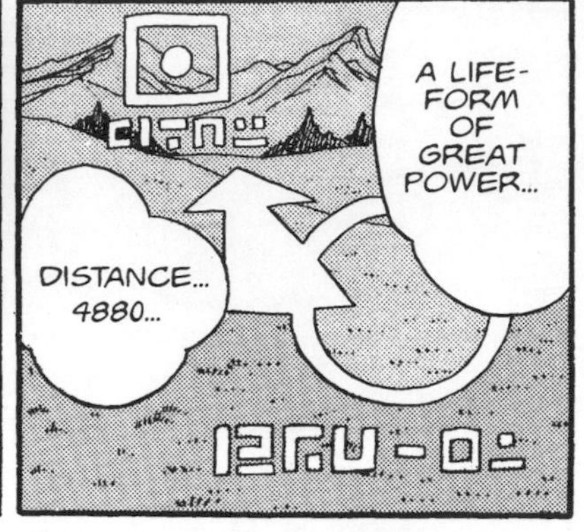
A LIFE-FORM OF GREAT POWER...
DISTANCE... 4880...

KAKARROT ?!

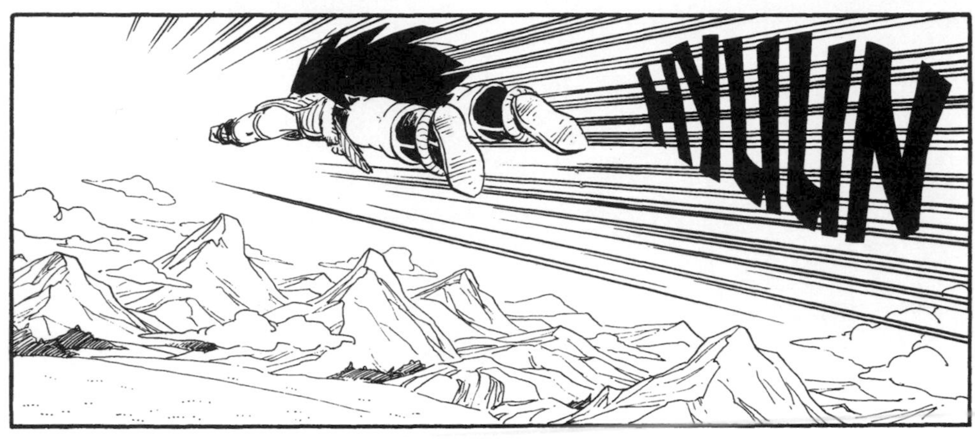
HYUUN

!!

I SENSE... A GREAT POWER...
COMING... CLOSER...!

IS IT SON GOKU ?!
HWOOOOOO

SSSHHHHH

NO !!!

FFT

FEH. YOU ARE NOT KAKARROT...

AND WHAT BEING ARE YOU?!
HAVE YOU BUSINESS WITH ME?

WITH THE LIKES OF YOU? NO.
THEN WHY DO YOU COME HERE?! WISH YOU TO DIE?!

HEH HEH HEH...
eep
QUITE THE FEISTY ONE, AREN'T YOU?

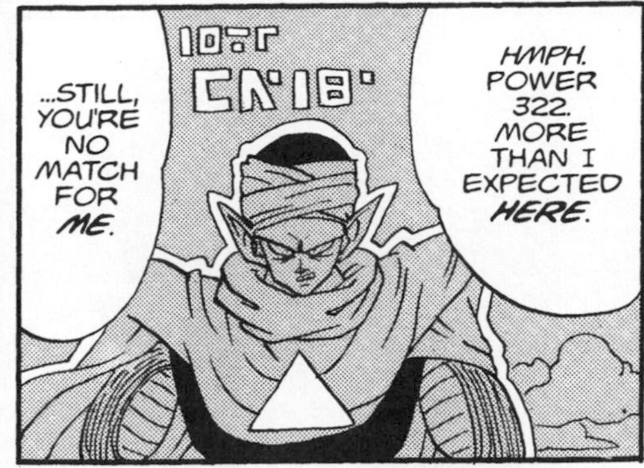
HMPH. POWER 322. MORE THAN I EXPECTED *HERE*.
...STILL, YOU'RE NO MATCH FOR *ME*.

WHAT SAY YOU?! KNOW YOU NOT THE ONE TO WHOM YOU SHOW SUCH *INSOLENCE* ?!
DO I CARE ?

THINKS HE HIMSELF *THAT* POWER-FUL...?

A FINE DISPLAY OF DUST, IF SUCH WAS YOUR INTENTION...

IS IT MY TURN ?
MAY I SHOW YOU SOME **REAL** POWER NOW...?

eep-
eep-
eep...
!

ANOTHER INCOMING POWER... A GREATER ONE...!

WHHHOOOO
?!

eep-
eep...
...AHA! ***THAT*** WAY! DISTANCE... 12909...

VAST POWER... THE GREATEST ON THIS WORLD...
CAN IT BE ANYONE OTHER THAN KAKARROT ?!

HYUUNNN

HUHH... HUHH...
THMP

IM...
IMPOSSIBLE...
I WAS PETRIFIED...
PARALYZED...

HAVE YOU LOST YOUR *PRIDE*... THE PRIDE OF THE *SAIYAN WARRIORS*...
...KAKARROT?!!

DBZ:02 · Kakarrot

KAME HOUSE

YO, ANYONE HOME...?

*KAME (PRONOUNCED "KAHMEH") IS THE JAPANESE WORD FOR "TURTLE," AS IN KAME-SEN'NIN, THE "TURTLE HERMIT."

BULMA!
OHH!

LONG TIME NO SEE!

IT'S BEEN TOO LONG, TOO LONG!
COLD ONE, AINTCHA? Y'NEVER COME OVER 'NLESS WE ASK YOU!
YEAH, WELL...

I'M HERE
NOW,
AREN'T I?
BEARING
TEA
CAKES,
EVEN.
CAKES,
YET
!

NOW WHY'D
YOU GO
AN' DO
A THING
LIKE THAT
?!
I'D'VE BEEN
PERFECTLY
HAPPY
WITH A
NICE
BIG
KI—

GAN

STILL NO
SENSE
OF
HUMOR,
I SEE...
JUST AS
ORNERY
AS EVER,
I SEE...

HYUUUUNNN...

BY THE WAY, BULMA, WHERE'S YAMCHA?

YAMCHA?! THAT JERK?!
YOU THINK I CARE?! AFTER WHAT HE DID?! WELL, THINK AGAIN, PAL!!

I'M BETTER OFF WITHOUT HIM AND SO ARE YOU!!
GETTING ALONG AS WELL AS EVER, I SEE...

FORGET HIM. WHERE'S THAT "LUNCH" CHICK?
WENT CHASING TENSHINHAN FIVE YEARS AGO. HAVEN'T SEEN HER SINCE.

HYUUNNN
SEE IT?! THAT'S MASTER MUTEN'S HOUSE!*
KAME HOUSE

*AS IN MUTEN RŌSHI, THE MORE **SERIOUS** NAME BY WHICH THE TURTLE HERMIT IS KNOWN.

GWOOOOMMMMMM

THE POWER SOURCE IS MOVING AT A HIGH VELOCITY...
eep eep eep...
THIS TIME, KAKARROT, YOU ARE *MINE*!

HERE WE ARE!
TOMP

HEY THERE !

HUH ?
IT'S *GOKU* !!

HAH!
HE'S STOPPED !!
HE'S CLOSE !!

WE'RE BACK !!

SON !!
GOKU !!

BUT WHO'S THE KID...?
YOU START BABY-SITTING ?
HE'S MINE !

SAY WHAT ?!!!!
"YOURS" AS IN... YOURS ?!

YEAH, 'SWRONG WITH THAT?
SAY HI, SQUIRT !
H-HELLO!

UHHH...
H-HELLO...
HIS NAME'S SON GOHAN.

SON GOHAN ?!
YOUR LATE GRAND-FATHER'S NAME?!

YUP !
B-BUT WE HAD NO IDEA-
I-I-MEAN... YOU...SON GOKU... WITH A CHILD...

*AS PART OF THEIR HERITAGE, SAIYANS WITH TAILS CAN, WHEN THE CONDITIONS ARE RIGHT, CHANGE INTO GIANT MONKEY-APES! FOR MORE INFO, SEE **DRAGON BALL**, VOLUME 2.*

IS HE... UH... STRONG LIKE YOU, TOO?
TH- THAT IS, I MEAN...

...I KNOW HE'S GOT IT IN 'IM...
...BUT CHI-CHI HAS A FIT IF I TRY TO TRAIN HIM!

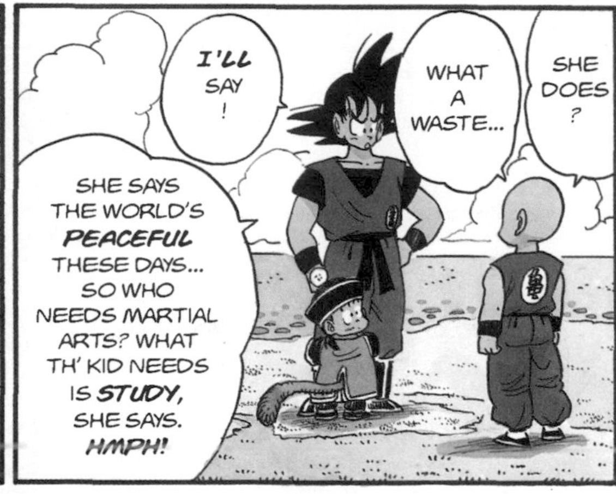

SHE DOES?
WHAT A WASTE...
I'LL SAY!
SHE SAYS THE WORLD'S PEACEFUL THESE DAYS... SO WHO NEEDS MARTIAL ARTS? WHAT TH' KID NEEDS IS STUDY, SHE SAYS. HMPH!

HAW HAW!
SO "DADDY'S LI'L GIRL" HAS TURNED INTA SUPER-MAMA, THEN, HAS SHE?!

HEY, I JUST NOTICED...IS THAT A DRAGON BALL ON GOHAN'S HAT...?

YUP! THE FOUR-STAR SŪSHINCHŪ!*
IT'S ALL I'VE GOT LEFT OF GRANDPA! I FOUND IT AN' PUT IT ON THERE.

I ALSO FOUND SANSHINCHŪ AND LIUSHINCHŪ... THREE-AND SIX-STAR. THEY'RE AT OUR PLACE.
DRAGON BALLS, HUH...? BOY, THOSE BRING BACK MEMORIES...

*THE SŪSHINCHŪ DRAGON BALL WAS GOKU'S ONLY KEEPSAKE OF HIS GRANDFATHER (SEE ***DRAGON BALL***, VOLUME 1, FOR DETAILS).

GASP

!!
HRRR!

WHAT IS IT, GOKU?! WHAT'S THE MATTER ?!
SOME-THING'S... COMING...
SOME-THING... STRONG !!

WHAT IS IT? I DON'T SEE-
BETTER NOT BE YAMCHA.

MUCH... MUCH MORE POWERFUL... SUPER POWERFUL... !!!
BUT WHAT... WHAT COULD POSSIBLY... ?

THERE!!!

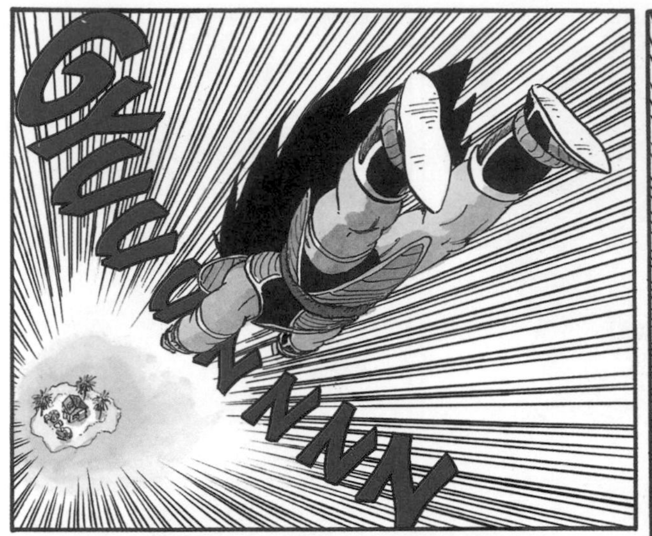
GYUUNNNN

AAH!!!

GASP!

TMM

MY, MY...ALL GROWN UP, ARE WE? STILL...I'D KNOW YOU ANYWHERE... ***KAKARROT.***

YOU LOOK... JUST LIKE YOUR FATHER.

HUH ?!
WHA... WHA'S HE TALKIN' ABOUT?
AND WHO IS HE?

HAS SOMETHING ON THIS WORLD ***DISTRACTED*** YOU, KAKARROT?
YOUR ***DUTY*** WAS TO ***EXTERMINATE*** THIS SPECIES!
WHAT GAME HAVE YOU BEEN PLAYING AT?!

LOOK, PAL...I DON'T KNOW WHO YOU ARE, BUT... ***GO HOME!*** *SCRAM! SHOO!*

THE ***LAST*** THING WE NEED IS DRUNKS LIKE ***YOU*** HANGIN' AROUND THE PLACE.

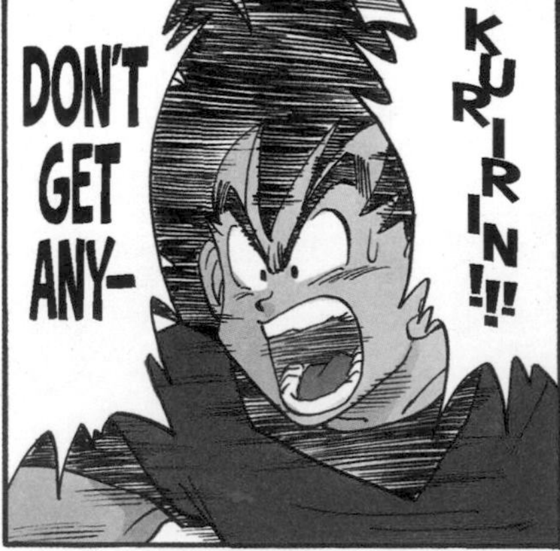

BWAK

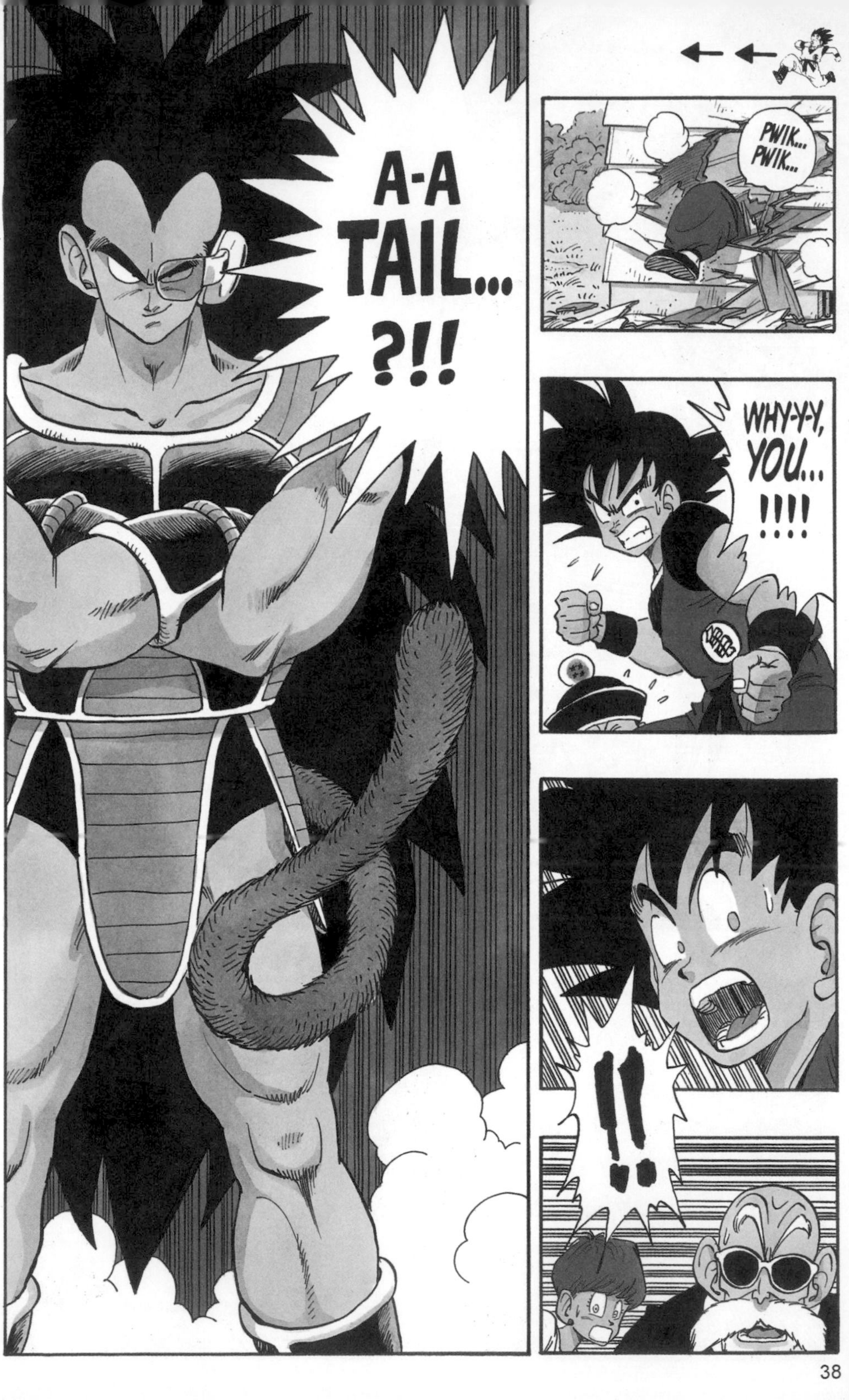

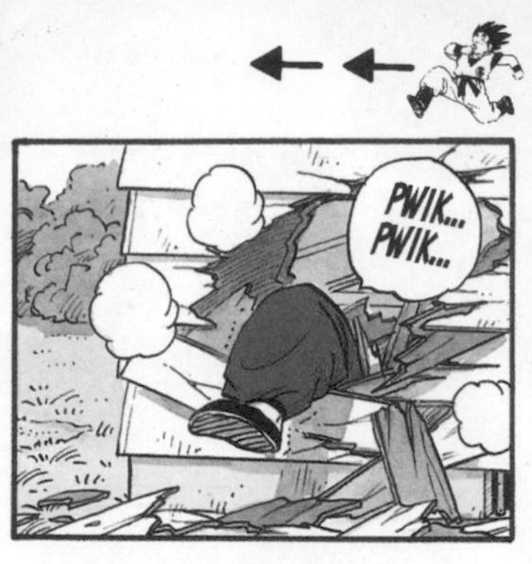
PWIK... PWIK...

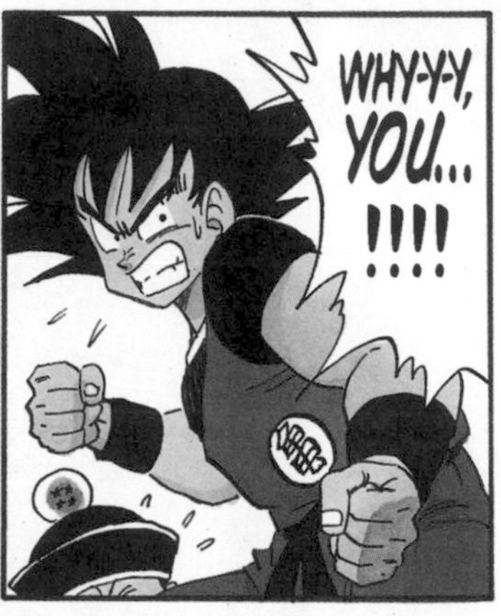
WHY-Y-Y, YOU... !!!!

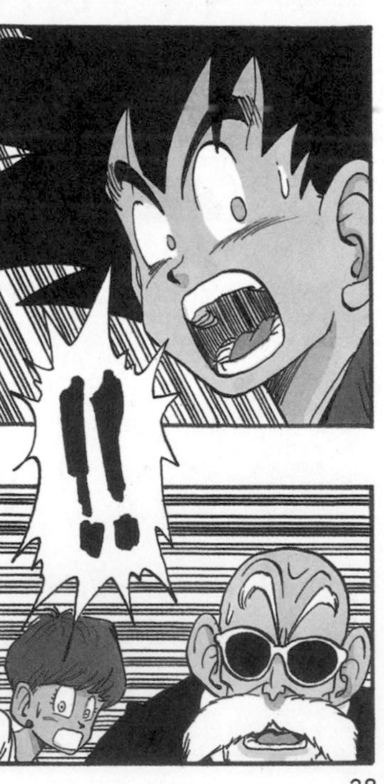
!!

A-A TAIL... ?!!

DBZ:03 · Tails of Future Not-Quite-Past

Y-
YOU'VE
GOT...
A
TAIL...!!
A TAIL...
JUST
LIKE *I*
USED TO
HAVE...!!

HEH
HEH
HEH...
SO NOW
THAT YOU
KNOW
WHO I
AM...

WHO
YOU
ARE...
?!
I *STILL*
DON'T GET
WHAT YOU
MEAN...!

IMPOSSIBLE! YOU COULD NEVER HAVE FORGOTTEN ME... OR OUR MISSION!
WHAT'S HAPPENED TO YOU, KAKARROT?! DID YOU TAKE A BLOW TO THE HEAD?!

LOOK, I DON'T KNOW WHO THIS "KAKA" GUY YOU'RE TALKING ABOUT IS...
...BUT I'M SON GOKU!!

YOU'RE INSANE!!
IT MUST BE A RESULT OF BRAIN DAMAGE!!

...OKAY! IT'S TRUE I'VE GOT A SCAR; MAYBE I DID HIT MY HEAD ONCE...
...BUT I WAS TOO LITTLE T' REMEMBER!

CURSE YOU, BUT THAT WOULD EXPLAIN IT...
EXPLAIN WHAT?! WHAT TH' HECK ARE YOU TALKIN' ABOUT?!

GOKU, YOUR GRANPA, SON GOHAN, HE... HE TOLD ME ONCE THAT HE FOUND A BABY IN THE WOODS, A BABY WITH A TAIL. HE WAS A WILD ONE, TOO, THAT BABY... ONE WHAT COULDN'T BE TAMED BY ANYONE...

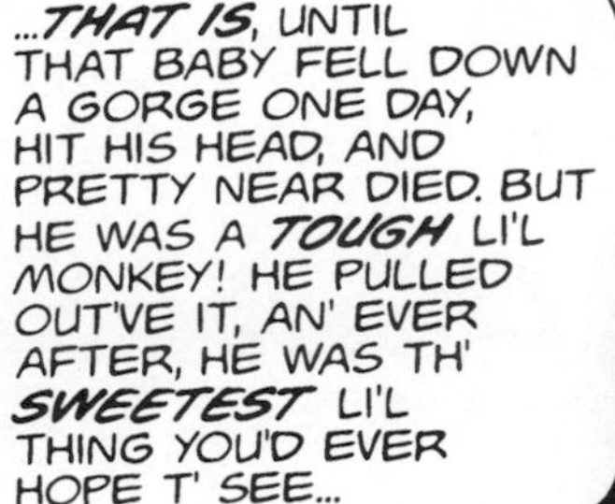

...THAT IS, UNTIL THAT BABY FELL DOWN A GORGE ONE DAY, HIT HIS HEAD, AND PRETTY NEAR DIED. BUT HE WAS A TOUGH LI'L MONKEY! HE PULLED OUT'VE IT, AN' EVER AFTER, HE WAS TH' SWEETEST LI'L THING YOU'D EVER HOPE T' SEE...

"SWEET" ?!
AN' THAT BABY... WAS ME?!
...HE WAS. IS.
.....

B-BUT WHAT'S THAT MEAN ?
WHO'S THAT GUY? AND WHAT'S HE GOT TO DO WITH GOKU?!
.....
ANSWER ME!! WHO ARE YOU?!
WHAT DO YOU WANT?!

TAKE WARNING— IF THERE IS ANY TRACE OF MEMORIES IN THERE, I WILL FIND A WAY TO REVEAL THEM!
SHRRRP
WE NEED YOU BACK, KAKARROT... YOUR PEOPLE NEED YOU BACK!

UNH...
OO-WAH...

KURIRIN! YOU OKAY?!
Y... YEAH...
BUT I DUNNO HOW...

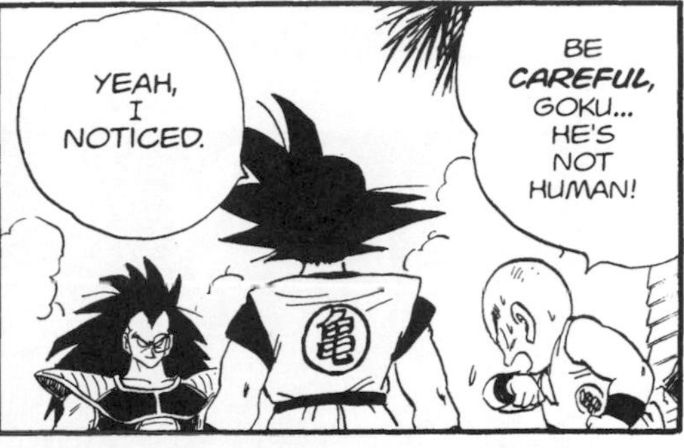

BE *CAREFUL,* GOKU... HE'S NOT HUMAN!
YEAH, I NOTICED.

JUST LOOKIN' AT HIM MAKES MY HAIR STAND ON END...
...AND THAT'S NEVER *HAPPENED* TO ME BEFORE!

THAT IS BECAUSE YOU AND I...WE ARE THE *SAME*!!

YOU ARE NO EARTHLING! YOU ARE A *SAIYAN WARRIOR*... A MEMBER OF THE MOST *POWERFUL RACE* IN THE *UNIVERSE*!!

!!

AND I AM RADITZ...
...YOUR OLDER BROTHER !!!

N-NO...
IT... IT CAN'T BE... !!!

KAME HOUSE
!!

G...G... G...G...
G-GOKU'S GOT A BROTHER... ?!

AND HE'S...AN ALIEN... ?!
N-NO WAY... !!

YOU LIAR!!
TAKE IT BACK!!
IF GOKU'S AN ALIEN, WHY'S HE HERE?!

HEH HEH HEH...

YOU MAY BE SORRY YOU ASKED, BUT THE ANSWER IS A SIMPLE ONE. WE ARE A WARRIOR RACE...AND AN ENTREPRENEURIAL ONE!
WE LOCATE HOSPITABLE PLANETS AND SELL THEM TO OTHER RACES LOOKING FOR LIVING SPACE. BUT, TO MAKE THOSE WORLDS SUITABLE TO THEIR FUTURE RESI-DENTS, FIRST WE MUST EXTERMINATE THE NATIVE INHABITANTS!

WHEN A SAIYAN WARRIOR IS FULLY GROWN, HE IS ASSIGNED TO THE MOST DIFFICULT WORLDS, THOSE WITH THE MOST POWERFUL NATIVES. BUT FIRST WE WARRIORS MUST HAVE YEARS OF PRACTICE. SO EVEN AS LITTLE CHILDREN, WE ARE, IN TIME, SENT TO DEPOPULATE THE ***WEAKER*** WORLDS...
WORLDS LIKE ***THIS*** ONE! IT'S A LUCKY THING THIS WORLD HAS A MOON...YOU'D HAVE WIPED OUT ALL THESE VERMIN WITHIN THE SPACE OF A FEW YEARS...***IF YOU HADN'T HIT YOUR SOFT LITTLE HEAD***!

IF...IF THIS IS ***TRUE***...TH-THEN ALL THESE THINGS, THEY...
...THEY MAKE ***PICCOLO*** LOOK LIKE THE BOY NEXT DOOR!! *

WAIT A MINUTE...
WHY IS IT "LUCKY" THAT EARTH HAS A MOON...?!

PICCOLO'S MANY EVIL DEEDS ARE SHOWN IN THE LATER VOLUMES OF ***DRAGON BALL*, WHICH TAKE PLACE BEFORE ***DRAGON BALL Z***.*

IS YOUR BRAIN ***THAT*** BADLY DAMAGED?! ONLY WHEN A MOON SHOWS ITS FULL FACE DO WE SAIYANS SHOW OUR TRUE POWERS!!

I'VE NO IDEA WHAT YOU'RE TALKING ABOUT!
THAT'S BECAUSE-

YOUR *TAIL*... !!
TELL ME, WHAT HAPPENED TO YOUR *TAIL*?!!
GOT CUT OFF A LONG TIME AGO. WHY?

NO *WONDER* YOU'VE BECOME SO COMFORTABLE IN THE WEAKLINGS' WORLD!
YOU'RE PASSING FOR ONE OF *THEM*... *YOU*, MY OWN BROTHER !!

SHUT UP!! I DON'T CARE IF YOU *ARE* MY BROTHER! I DON'T CARE IF I *AM* AN ALIEN!!
KURIRIN WAS *RIGHT*— PEOPLE LIKE YOU ARE JUST *WRONG*!!

I'M SON GOKU NOW!!
GET THE HECK OFF MY PLANET!!

YOU TELL 'IM, GOKU!
NURTURE OVER NATURE, M'BOY! GOKU'S NOT JUST AN EARTHLING... HE'S TH' BEST DANG EARTHLING I KNOW!
HE EVEN SAVED THIS PLANET ONCE! SO DO US A FAVOR AND JUST GO, WILL YA?!

HEH HEH HEH...
SERIOUSLY, THOUGH, HOW DO YOU EXPECT ME TO DO THAT...?

I SUPPOSE YOU'VE FORGOTTEN THAT VEGETA, THE SAIYAN HOMEWORLD, WAS DESTROYED BY COLLISION WITH AN ASTEROID...
OUR ENTIRE RACE WAS REDUCED TO SPACE DUST...

...EVEN OUR PARENTS. YOUR PARENTS, KAKARROT.

......

OF ALL OUR PROUD AND MIGHTY RACE, ONLY FOUR REMAIN... INCLUDING YOU!
WE SURVIVED ONLY BECAUSE WE WERE ON OTHER WORLDS... EXTERMINATING THEIR NATIVES. BECAUSE WE WERE DOING "WRONG," AS YOU PUT IT, WE ARE ALIVE!

WE REMAINING THREE RECENTLY FOUND A PLANET WHICH WE KNOW CAN BE SOLD AT A VERY HIGH PRICE. THE LOCALS, HOWEVER, ARE POTENT. EVEN THREE SAIYAN MIGHT HAVE SOME TROUBLE.
AH, BUT FOUR OF US...! THANK THE GODS I REMEMBERED YOU, EH? EVEN MY LONG-LOST, ILL-TRAINED, AMNESIAC LITTLE BROTHER SHOULD BE ENOUGH TO TIP THE SCALES.

PICTURE IT, KAKARROT!!!
PICTURE THE CARNAGE! FEEL YOUR SAIYAN BLOOD STIR!!

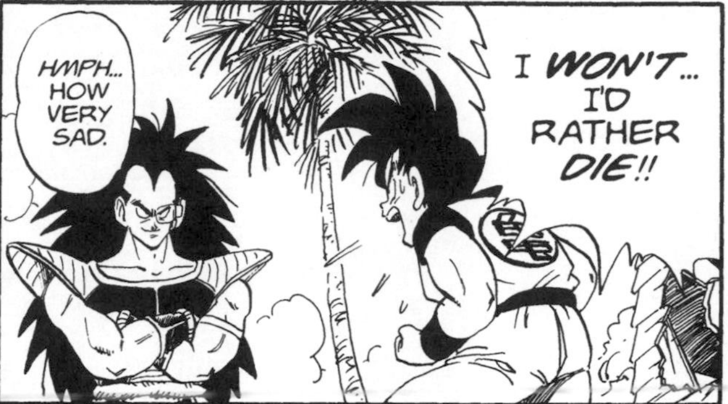
I WON'T... I'D RATHER DIE!!
HMPH... HOW VERY SAD.

BUT DO TELL ME SOME-THING...
...IS THAT YOUR WHELP I SEE BEHIND YOU?

!!
N-NO!!!
OH, IS THAT SO...?
I SUPPOSE ALL MISERABLE EARTHLINGS HAVE TAILS, THEN...?

YOU LEAVE HIM ALONE!!!

SORRY. CAN'T BE DONE. IF MY OWN BROTHER WON'T DEIGN TO HELP ME...
...THEN I'LL JUST HAVE TO BORROW MY TENDER YOUNG NEPHEW INSTEAD...

ONE MORE **STEP,** AND I'LL **KILL** YOU!!!
SHK
SHK

FSH

...NGH...!!
NNG... GGUHH...!!

FUDD

DADDY-Y-Y !!
.....
OH, NO YOU DON'T.

IF YOU WISH HIM RETURNED TO YOU *ALIVE*, KAKARROT...
...YOU WILL FOLLOW MY ORDERS... IS THAT CLEAR?
BWAAAH!!!

RRR... GUHH... !
HE...HE BEAT GOKU...
W-WITH *ONE KICK*, YET...

I'LL GIVE YOU A FULL EARTH DAY TO... SHALL WE SAY... AGONIZE OVER IT.
WHEN YOU DECIDE TO JOIN US... AND YOU *WILL* DECIDE THAT... WE SHALL REQUIRE... PROOF...OF YOUR GOOD INTENTIONS.

LET'S MAKE IT SIMPLE.
A HUNDRED HUMANS BY THIS TIME TOMORROW. PILE THE BODIES HERE, AND DON'T THINK WE WON'T COUNT.

DID YOU HEAR ME? I'LL BE LOOKING FORWARD TO TOMORROW.
THIS IS, AFTER ALL, MY ONLY NEPHEW...I'D HATE TO HAVE TO KILL HIM.

Y-YOU *WOULDN'T*...
Y-YOU *CAN'T-* !!

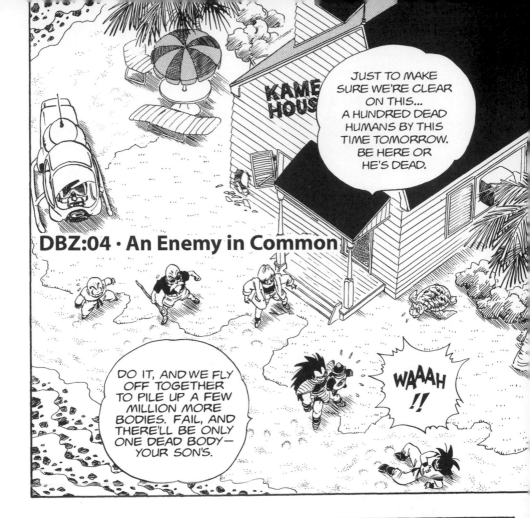

DBZ:04 · An Enemy in Common

JUST TO MAKE SURE WE'RE CLEAR ON THIS... A HUNDRED DEAD HUMANS BY THIS TIME TOMORROW. BE HERE OR HE'S DEAD.

DO IT, AND WE FLY OFF TOGETHER TO PILE UP A FEW MILLION MORE BODIES. FAIL, AND THERE'LL BE ONLY ONE DEAD BODY—YOUR SON'S.

WAAAH!!

H-HE'S RIGHT! IF YOU THINK GOKU'D EVER GO 'N' KILL SOMEBODY, YOU'RE CRAZY!!
Y-YOU CALL YOURSELF A WARRIOR?! USIN' A *KID*...?!
UNGH... !

THE CHOICE IS HIS.
IF HE VALUES A HUNDRED HUMANS OVER HIS SON, FINE.

ALTHOUGH, I FEEL I SHOULD WARN YOU, AFTER MY COMRADES AND I EXTERMINATE THE VERMIN ON THAT OTHER WORLD...
...WE MOST CERTAINLY SHALL RETURN AND REPEAT THE PROCESS HERE!

WHAT ?!
Y-YOU'LL WH- WHA— ?!!

I GIVE THE INHABITANTS OF YOUR PUNY PLANET...OH, LET'S SAY A ***MONTH***... ONCE WE THREE BEGIN THE CLEAN-UP PROCESS...
REALLY, IF YOU THINK ABOUT IT, WHAT DIFFERENCE WOULD IT MAKE IF KAKARROT SHOULD HAPPEN TO GIVE ONE HUNDRED OF YOU A HEAD START...?

DO YOU ***SEE*** NOW?! YOUR "CHOICE" IS ***NO*** CHOICE AT ALL, MY DEAR YOUNGER BROTHER!!
GIVE ME... BACK...MY... ***SON***...!!

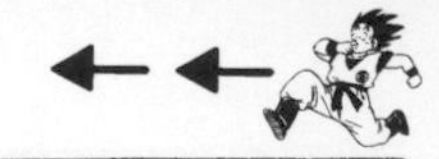

MAKE THE *RIGHT* DECISION, MY BROTHER...
...FOR *YOUR* SAKE, AS WELL AS HIS!

......

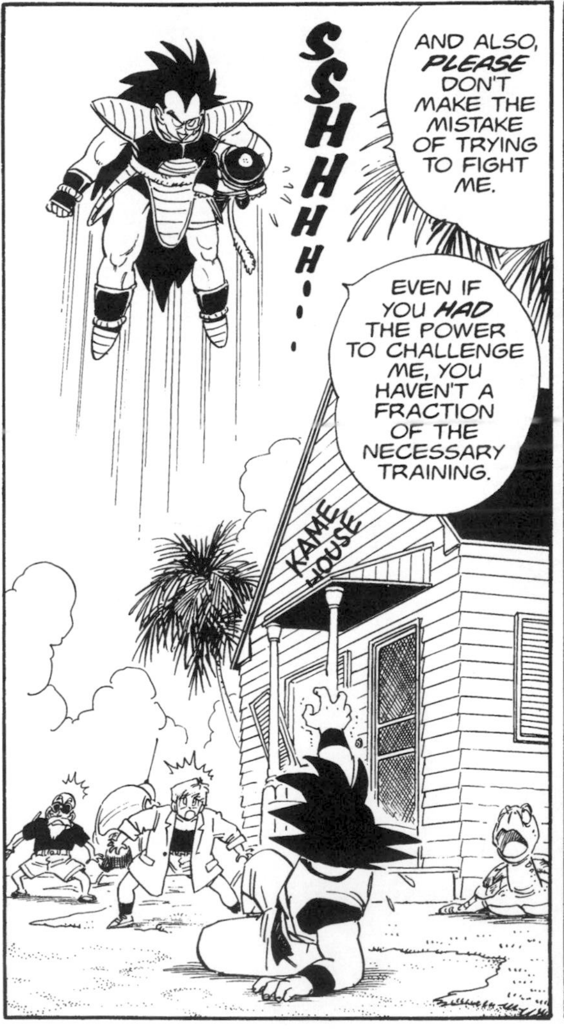

AND ALSO, *PLEASE* DON'T MAKE THE MISTAKE OF TRYING TO FIGHT ME.
SSHHHH...
EVEN IF YOU *HAD* THE POWER TO CHALLENGE ME, YOU HAVEN'T A FRACTION OF THE NECESSARY TRAINING.
KAME HOUSE

DAA-
A-A-
D-D-
Y-Y-Y—
!!!

G-GO-O-O-
HA-A-A-N
!!!

UNTIL TOMORROW, "KAKARROT"... !!

GYUUUNNNNNN
WA HA HA HA HA !!!

YOU...
...CAN'T... DO... THIS!!
DMM

Y-YOU CAN'T... DO THIS...
GOKU! GOKU, ARE YOU OKAY?!
I'M SORRY, LAD... W-WE COULDN'T HELP...

K-KINTO'UN!!! TO *ME*!!

WAIT!!! DON'T GO RUNNIN' OFF HALF-COCKED!!!
Y-YOU *CAN'T*!! YOU'LL BE *KILLED*!!

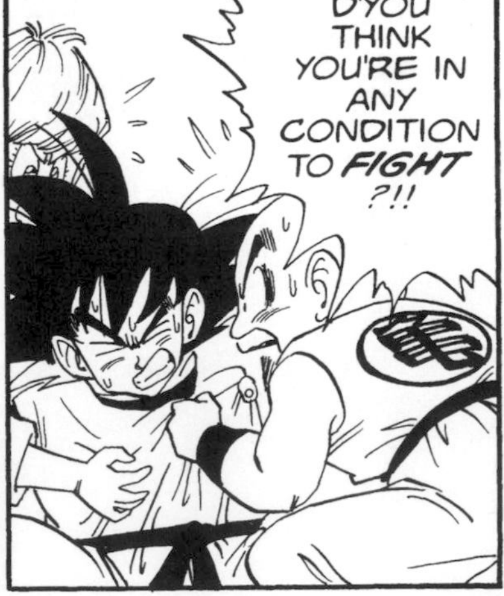
D'YOU THINK YOU'RE IN ANY CONDITION TO *FIGHT*?!!

B-BUT I...I'VE GOTTA DO *SOME-THING*...
THEN LET'S THINK...

HOW AWFUL...! FINDING YOUR FAMILY AFTER ALL THIS TIME, AND THEN...TO FIND OUT IT'S SOMEONE LIKE HIM...

I-IT DOESN'T MATTER...
NO MATTER WHO HE IS, I'LL NEVER FORGIVE HIM...

SO, THEN... WHAT'RE YOU GONNA DO?
I'VE NEVER SEEN ANYBODY THAT STRONG...
I-I MEAN, IF HE CAN EVEN TAKE YOU DOWN...

...HIS TAIL.
HIS WEAKNESS IS HIS TAIL, AN' IF HE'S GOT THE SAME WEAKNESS I DID...
...ALL I GOTTA DO IS CRUSH IT...

...AND HIS POWER'LL DROP.
N-NOW THAT Y' MENTION IT...
THAT'S FINE, BUT... HOW THE HECK'RE YOU GONNA GET TO IT?!

I CAN'T. ...THAT IS, NOT BY MYSELF.
GLAK

NOW WE'RE TALKIN'!! DON' YOU WORRY, SON— WE'LL HELP THE BEST WE CAN.
'COURSE, NO ONE KNOWS THE WHEREABOUTS OF YAMCHA OR TENSHINHAN, BUT...
B-BUT IF TH-THE TH-TH-THREE'VE US F-FUH-FIGHT T'GETHER...
WE'RE ALL GONNA DIE...

BUT, HEY! IF WE ALL BUY IT, BULMA CAN USE TH' DRAGON BALLS TO BRING US ALL BACK, RIGHT??
THUMP!
LEAVE IT TO ME!

NO, KURIRIN...SHE CAN'T! I FOUND OUT THAT SHENLONG NEVER GRANTS THE SAME WISH TWICE...
...AND YOU AN' KAME-SEN'NIN HAVE ALREADY BEEN BROUGHT BACK TO LIFE! THIS TIME... DEATH MEANS DEATH!!

.....
I, UH... YEAH, HUH?

YOU'LL STILL HELP ME THO', RIGHT?
'C-COURSE WE WILL, EH, BOY??
S-SURE, W-WI-WITHOUT A M-MUH-MOMENT'S DOUBT!!

"DEATH MEANS DEATH," HUH...?
I'LL NEVER GET A GIRL-FRIEND AT THIS RATE...

SPEAKING OF DRAGON BALLS, HOW'S THIS FOR AN IDEA?? WHY DONTCHA GET ALL SEVEN TOGETHER AND TELL SHENLONG "SAVE THE WORLD!" OR WHATEVER?!
BULMA, YOU'RE A GENIUS!!

THINKIN' T' FIND ALL SEVEN IN ONE DAY, EH, SON...?
OH... RIGHT...

ALL RIGHT, THEN! HE WON'T BE EXPECTING AN ATTACK.
WE SHOULD BE ABLE TO CATCH HIM OFF-GUARD, NO PROBLEM.
B-BUT, WE DON'T EVEN KNOW WHERE HE'S AT, PLUS—

BULMA!! YOU STILL CARRYIN' THAT DRAGON RADAR ??
YOU'RE ***RIGHT***!! GOHAN'S ***HAT***!! THERE'S A ***DRAGON BALL*** ON IT, ISN'T THERE?

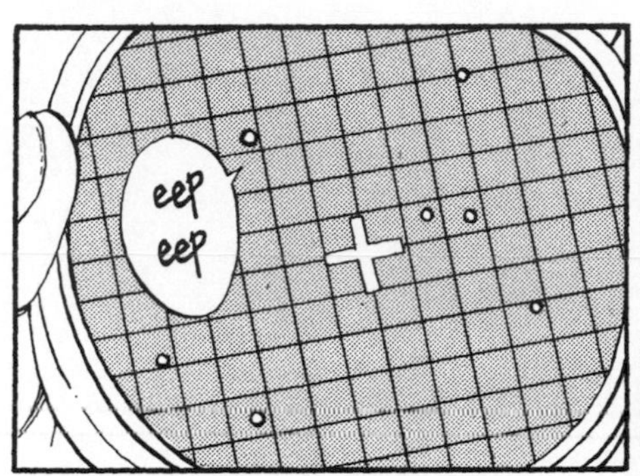
eep eep

THERE!! MOVING ***INCREDIBLY*** FAST!!
WHERE'S HE HEADIN', I WONDER... ?

IT STOPPED !!!
THANK GOODNESS! HE'S STAYING ON EARTH!!

"GOOD" IS ***RIGHT***! GOOD FOR HIM... GOOD FOR ***US***!!
W-WE MAY EVEN HAVE A CHANCE'VE ***WINNIN'*** THIS THING!!
NOT ***MUCH***'VE A CHANCE, BUT...
ALWAYS BETTER T' DIE FEELIN' OPTIMISTIC, OR SO ***I*** ALWAYS SAY...

YOU HAVEN'T A CHANCE...
WHA- ?!

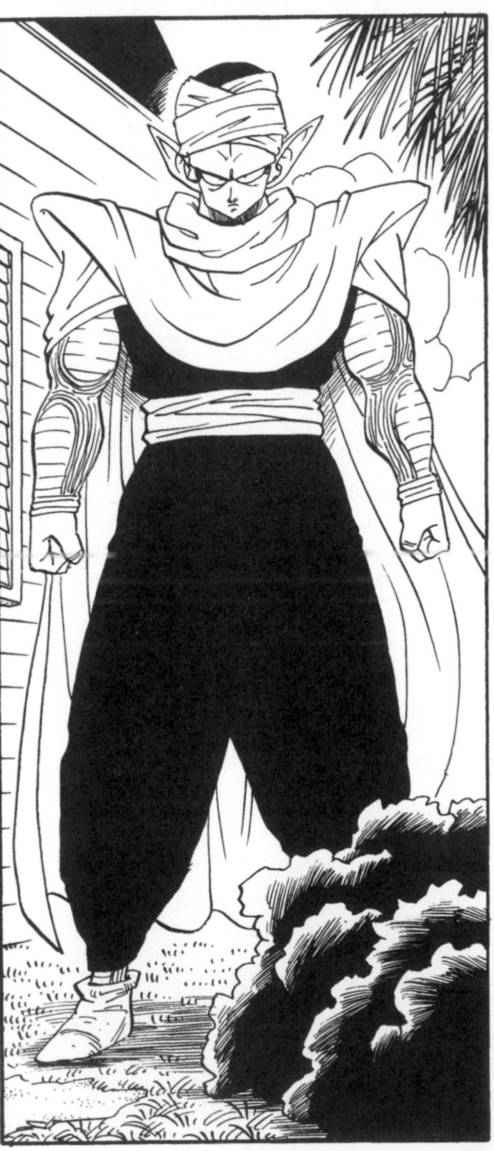

PICCOLO !!!

AND WHAT ARE *YOU* DOING HERE?!
...I WANT *HIM*.
EEEE-YAAA !!

YOU TWO KNOW EACH OTHER, HUH? FIGURES.
HE AND I HAVE... MET.

AND YOU THREE HAVE NOT A PRAYER AGAINST HIM.
PLACE YOUR HOPES IN *ME*, OR PLACE THEM NOT AT ALL...

KNOW YOU WELL HIS STRENGTH SURPASSES THAT OF YOU OR I...

ALONE, WE FIND OURSELVES EQUALLY OUT-MATCHED...
TOGETHER, HOWEVER, OUR POWERS MAY PROVE JUST STRONG ENOUGH!!

...COULD BE.
MIND TELLING ME WHAT'S IN IT FOR YOU?

I BEAR YOU NO LOVE, THAT MUCH IS TRUE.
AND WHETHER YOUR SON LIVES OR DIES IS A MATTER BENEATH MY NOTICE...
BUT I HAVE PLANS FOR THIS WORLD, AND I WILL ALLOW NO ONE TO INTERFERE!

THE MOMENT AFTER WE USE OUR COMBINED POWERS TO DESTROY THIS RAGGEDY SAIYAN...
...I TURN MY POWERS ON YOU... AND THIS TIME, THE EARTH SHALL BE MINE!!

AFTER THAT, THO', ALL BETS ARE OFF!
YOU'RE WELCOME TO TRY.
AND I INTEND TO PLAY ALONG UNTIL MY BOY IS SAFE...
SO BE IT.
I PRAY ONLY THAT I MAY CONTAIN MY NAUSEA AT THE THOUGHT OF JOINING WITH YOU...

BULMA! GIMME THE RADAR !!
HUH? WHA?? O-OKAY...

SHUMP

HEY, PIC! CAN YA KEEP UP WITH MY CLOUD ?!
SPARE ME YOUR FOLLY.
THE SPEED OF MY FLIGHT WILL SPEAK FOR ITSELF.

ZHMMM

......

A-ARE WE SUPPOSED TO BE *HAPPY*, OR...?

DUNNO 'BOUT "HAPPY"...
B-BUMP
B-BUMP
...BUT IF THOSE TWO ARE JOININ' FORCES, YOU CAN BET...

...WE'RE ALL IN FOR ONE HECKUVA *FRACAS* !!
HECK, THEY MAY EVEN *WIN* TH' DARN THING!

I, FOR ONE, DON' INTEND TO *MISS* IT!!
BULMA!! WHERE'S THAT RADAR THINGAMAJIG POINTIN' AT?!
WE'RE GOIN' ALONG FOR TH' RIDE!!

DBZ:05 · An Unexpected Strength

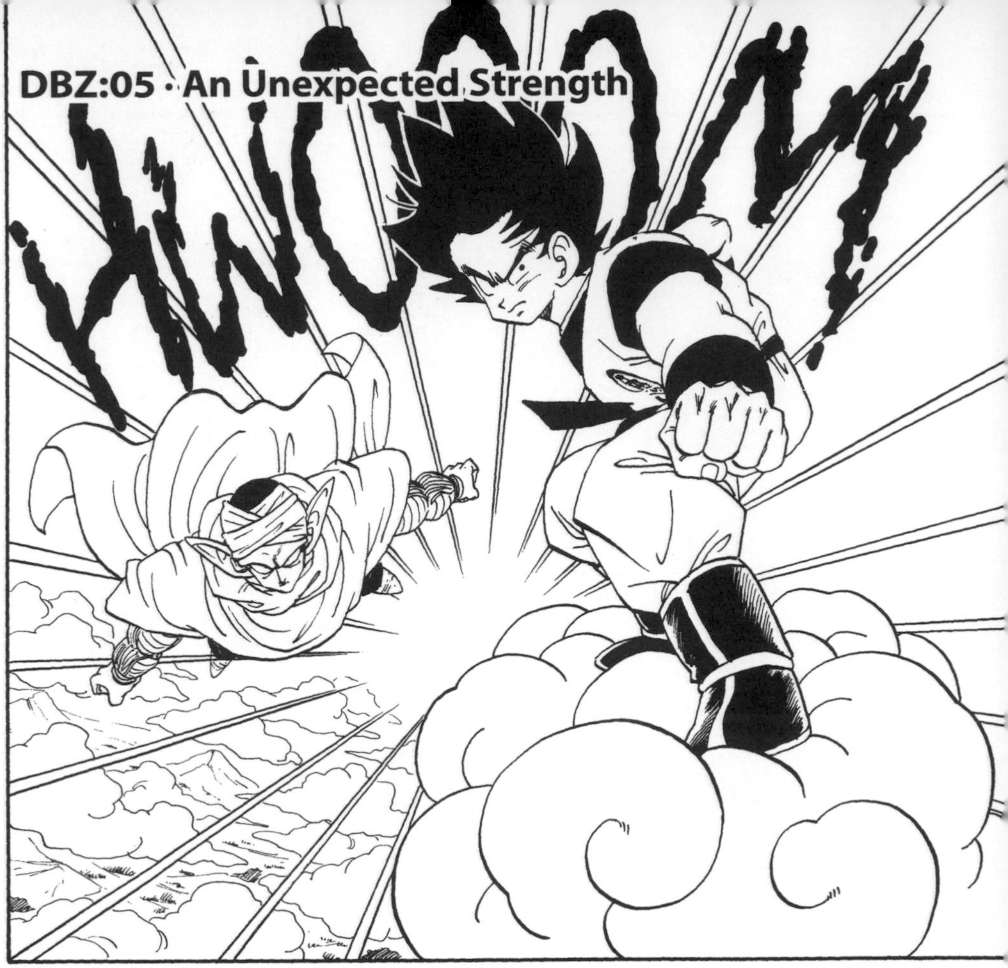

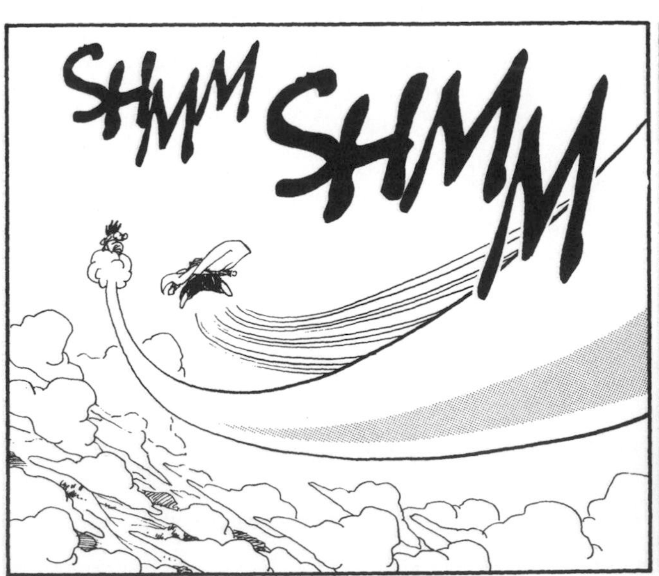
SHMM SHMM

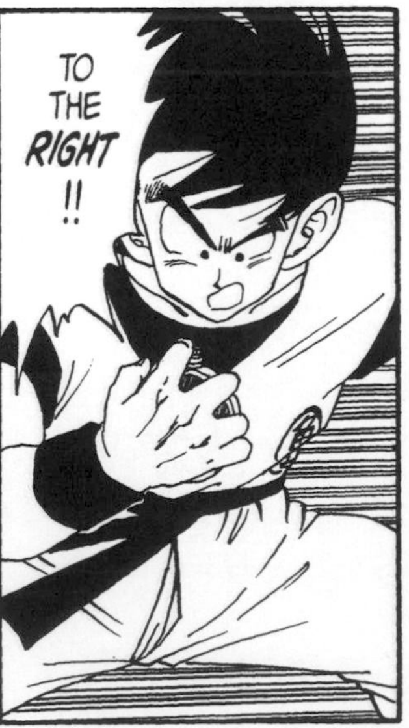
TO THE RIGHT !!

WAAA WAAA
STOP BAWLING, CHILD!
THE BLOOD OF *SAIYANS* RUNS THROUGH YOU !!

YOU'LL STAY IN HERE!

BLANG..

NEXT...
...THE NEEDS OF THE BODY MUST BE MET.

PIIIP
MM?

STRANGE...
KCH
AN ALERT...? BUT...

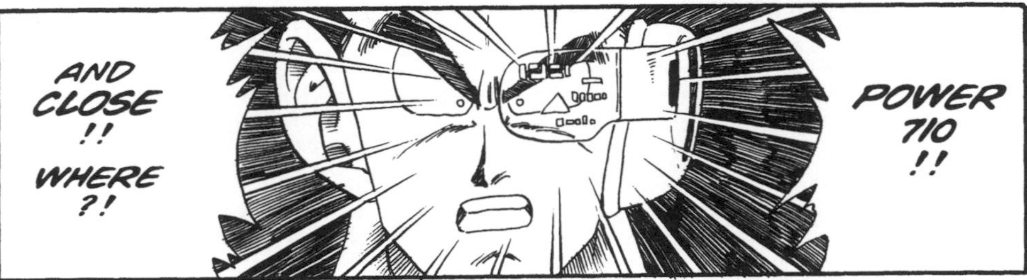
POWER 710!!
AND CLOSE!! WHERE?!

PI PI PI...
PIIIIII

WHAT?!
THAT... INFANT?!

BLASTED TECHNOLOGY...
THIS IS NO TIME TO MAL-FUNCTION!

WE'RE CLOSE !!
WE'D BETTER START GOING LOWER-

IT SHALL MAKE NO DIF- FERENCE !!
WHAT ?!

HE HOLDS A DEVICE THAT REVEALS...
...AN OPPONENT'S POSITION... AND HIS POWER !!

Y'MEAN...
HE KNOWS... ?
THAT WE ARE COMING? YES.

IN THAT CASE...
...THERE'S NOTHING TO DO BUT HIT HIM HEAD ON!!

POWER 710...
WHAT AILS THIS DEVICE...?

PI PI!
A NEW READING...

—INCOMING QUICKLY!

PI PI!!
—AGAIN!

ONE... NO, *TWO* OF THEM...
POWERS 322 AND 334!
ONE HAS KAKARROT'S POWER... EXACTLY.

BUT WOULD HE *DARE* TO CHALLENGE ME AGAIN, KNOWING HE HAS NO HOPE?
AND HOW WOULD HE FIND ME...?

THIS WORTHLESS GADGET...
I NEEDN'T KEEP *IT* ANY—

—IT CAN'T BE !!
!!

IT IS HIM !!

FOR A CHILD, EVEN THE CHILD OF A *SAIYAN,* TO HAVE A POWER LEVEL OF 710—

CAN IT BE THE SCOPE IS *NOT* BROKEN ??

HSHH

TMP

TMP

I SEE.
YOU'VE FOUND A COMMON CAUSE.

AND HOW DID YOU FIND *ME*?
WE *DID*. THAT'S ALL.

FINE. THEN LET'S TRY ANOTHER QUESTION...
WHY DID YOU WANT TO FIND ME?

WHY DO YOU *THINK* ?!
TO TAKE BACK MY *SON*!!

THEN YOU STILL REFUSE TO AFFIRM YOUR SAIYAN BIRTH BY JOINING US?
GIVE ME MY *SON* !

EVEN IF IT MEANS DISOBEYING YOUR OWN BROTHER ?

I DON'T *HAVE* A BROTHER !

REALLY, KAKARROT... I EXPECTED MUCH BETTER THINGS OF YOU.
HOW CAN A *SAIYAN* BE SUCH A *FOOL*?

SURELY YOU DON'T IMAGINE THAT EVEN THE TWO OF YOU TOGETHER CAN DEFEAT *ME*...?

FWA
RADITZ... YOU TALK TOO MUCH.

DNG

PICCOLO... YOU WERE ARMORED, TOO?
AS ARE YOU, BOY...

AND I HAVE NOT FELT SO LIGHT IN A LONG WHILE...

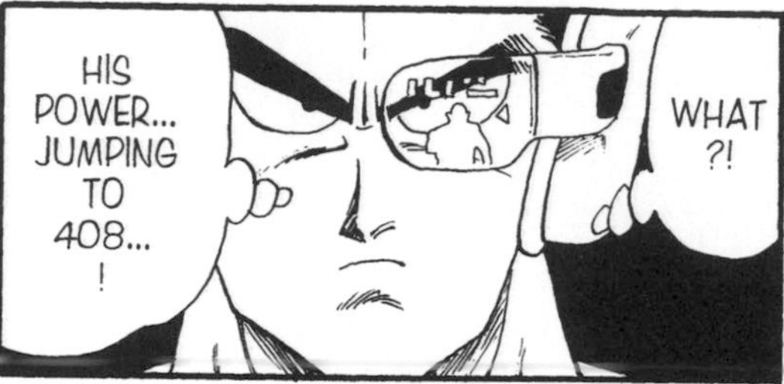
WHAT ?!
HIS POWER... JUMPING TO 408... !

WELL, WELL...
LOOKS LIKE WE'VE BOTH BEEN TRAINING HARD!

ANYWAY, I'M JUST GLAD...
...THAT *THIS* TIME, YOU'RE ON *MY* SIDE.

THIS...IS GONNA BE A *FIGHT*!

AND KAKARROT... UP TO 416...!

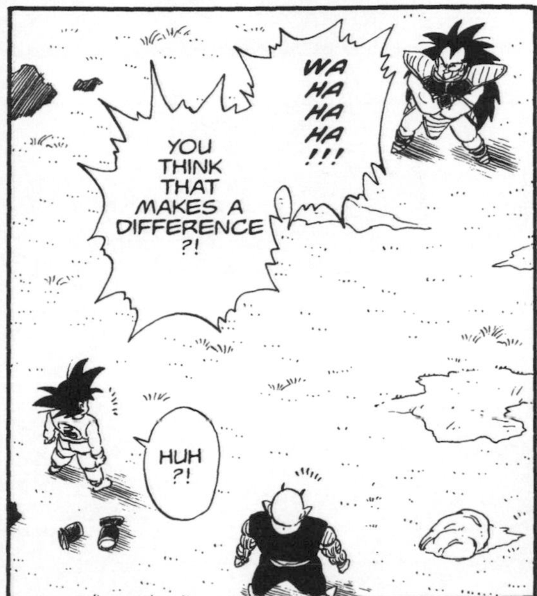
WA HA HA HA!!!
YOU THINK THAT MAKES A DIFFERENCE?!
HUH?!

ADD *HUNDREDS* MORE DEGREES, THE *BOTH* OF YOU!!
YOU'LL *STILL* BE NO MATCH FOR *ME*!!

IF YOU THINK POWER IS EVERYTHING...
...THEN YOU'RE NO FIGHTER!

YOUTH I MIGHT FORGIVE...
...BUT IDIOCY HAS NO PLACE ON A SAIYAN MISSION, KAKARROT.

YOU ARE A SHAME TO OUR RACE!!
YOU WILL DIE!!!!

VM
!!
B-BAM

BWA
PM

HE... HE'S **FAST** !!
SO FAST I CAN HARDLY **BELIEVE** IT!!

HE CHARGED FROM THE FORE...
...YET HIS BLOWS STRUCK OUR **BACKS** !

WELL. YOUR DEFENSES AREN'T BAD.

THAT WILL KEEP YOU ALIVE A FEW MORE MINUTES...
...AS I INCREASE THE POWER OF MY ATTACKS.

HE SHOWED NO SUCH POWER AS *THIS* BEFORE...

HIS STRENGTH'S IN HIS TAIL...BUT HOW DO WE GET TO IT...?

...OH, ONE MORE THING. SHOULD YOU STILL HOPE TO *WIN*, YOU SHOULD KNOW...

THE OTHER SAIYANS... MY TWO PARTNERS...
...ARE *BOTH* SUPERIOR TO ME IN STRENGTH.

HA HA HA HA HA!!!

HOW DO YOU LIKE THE TASTE OF *DESPAIR*, EH?!!

DBZ:06 • Nothing Up My Sleeve...

IT IS THE LAST TASTE YOU FOOLS WILL EVER KNOW...

AND SO... SHOULD WE SUCCEED IN STRIKING YOU DOWN...
WE FACE TWICE YOUR POWER... AND MORE...

Y'KNOW, PICCOLO...
...I COULDA *WAITED* TO HEAR THAT.

DOES IT NOT THRILL YOU, SON GOKU...?
HEH... "THRILL" PROBABLY ISN'T THE WORD I'D PICK...
"SPITLESS" MIGHT BE A BETTER ONE...OR "TERRIFIED"...

STILL, I WILL TAKE BACK MY SON!
WHERE DID YOU HIDE HIM?!

"HIDE," INDEED. I LOCKED HIM UP TO KEEP HIM QUIET.
HE'S IN THAT HOLE BEHIND YOU. AND STILL ALIVE... PROBABLY.

...
SSS...

THERE... !
DADDY'S HERE, GOHAN !!!
HANG IN THERE, OKAY?! DADDY'LL SAVE YOU!!

HA HAAA! DON'T GET THE POOR LAD'S HOPES UP!!
NO DEAD DADDY WILL BE SAVING HIM!!!

TMP

PICCOLO... READY ?!
HAVE WE A CHOICE... ?!

HIII- YAAA !!!!!

SH
PA
PA
PA

PM
PM

SHP

KR-KRAK

DMM

DMM

fff
VWP
VWP

GRRR!!!

BM!
BM

SHP
HWOOOOOO

BOOM

!!
AAUGH!!
GWMM

YAAA!!
SHMM
DKOOM

DDOOMM

HSST

THP

BEHIND YOU!
HNGH!!!

BWAK
ZZHHH

UH... UHH...

HEH HEH HEH...
DO YOU BELIEVE ME NOW...?

NN... NNKH...!

HUH
HUH
AGH...
P-PICCOLO... ARE YOU...?

!!

...HEHH...
QUITE... AN INCONVENIENCE...
...HAVING TO FIGHT... WITH ONE ARM...

WA HA HA !!!!
I'LL TAKE YOUR WRETCHED *HEAD* NEXT !!!

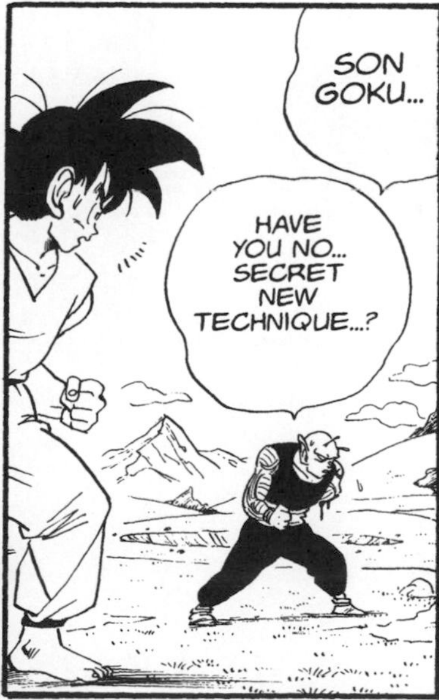
SON GOKU...
HAVE YOU NO... SECRET NEW TECHNIQUE...?

HEH... FOR ONCE, PICCOLO...
...I'M FRESH OUT.

YOU ALWAYS WERE... A LAZY ONE...
WE SHOULD BOTH BE THANKFUL... THAT I AM *NOT*...

DBZ:07 • Piccolo's Farewell to Arms?!

MAKING SECRET ***PLANS***, LITTLE FRIENDS?

WELL, IF THAT'S HOW YOU CHOOSE TO WASTE THE LAST MOMENTS OF YOUR LIVES... ENJOY YOURSELVES! *WA HA HA!*

ARE YOU SAYING YOU'VE GOT A NEW TECH-NIQUE...?
PSSS PSSSS...
INDEED...

CAN YOU DO IT WITH ONE ARM?

THE LACK OF A LIMB...WILL BE NO OBSTACLE... BUT I REQUIRE TIME TO CONCENTRATE MY POWER...
...AND SO I REQUIRE ***YOU***...TO KEEP HIM OCCUPIED ALONE...

YOU'D BETTER BE SURE IT'S GONNA WORK...

CERTAINTY... IS NOT THE LOT OF WE MERE MORTALS... BUT WHAT CHOICE DO WE HAVE...?
SUCH A PITY, THOUGH...I DEVISED THIS TECHNIQUE ESPECIALLY TO KILL *YOU*...

ONCE THIS CREATURE IS FELLED... YOUR TURN WILL COME...
...BUT IT'LL *HELP* ME INSTEAD. I LIKE THAT!

HA HA HA...
LIFE... NEVER FAILS TO AMUSE... EH?

LAUGHING...
ARE THEY INSANE... ?!

ALL RIGHT!! DO WHAT YOU'VE GOTTA DO!!
I'LL KEEP HIM *BUSY* !!

HOLD HIM...AS LONG AS YOU CAN...!

DM

LIGHT... OF DEATH !!!
SHA!

WOK
WOKK
WOK

HYAAA...!!

BBBB...

UNH !!!
BNNG
PERSIS-TENT WRETCH... !!

IT CAN'T BE!!! HIS POWER... UP TO 924!!!
AND INCREASING... !!

SOMEHOW... HE CAN FOCUS ALL HIS ENERGY INTO A SINGLE POINT...!!!

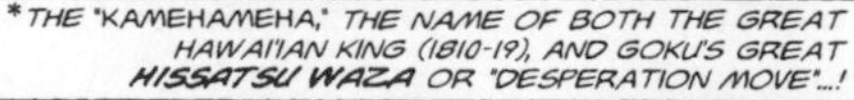
*THE "KAMEHAMEHA," THE NAME OF BOTH THE GREAT HAWAI'IAN KING (1810-19), AND GOKU'S GREAT ***HISSATSU WAZA*** OR "DESPERATION MOVE"...!

!!

THAT ONE... 1020...1030...!!!!
IT'S UNBELIEVABLE !!!!

HYAAA!!!!!!

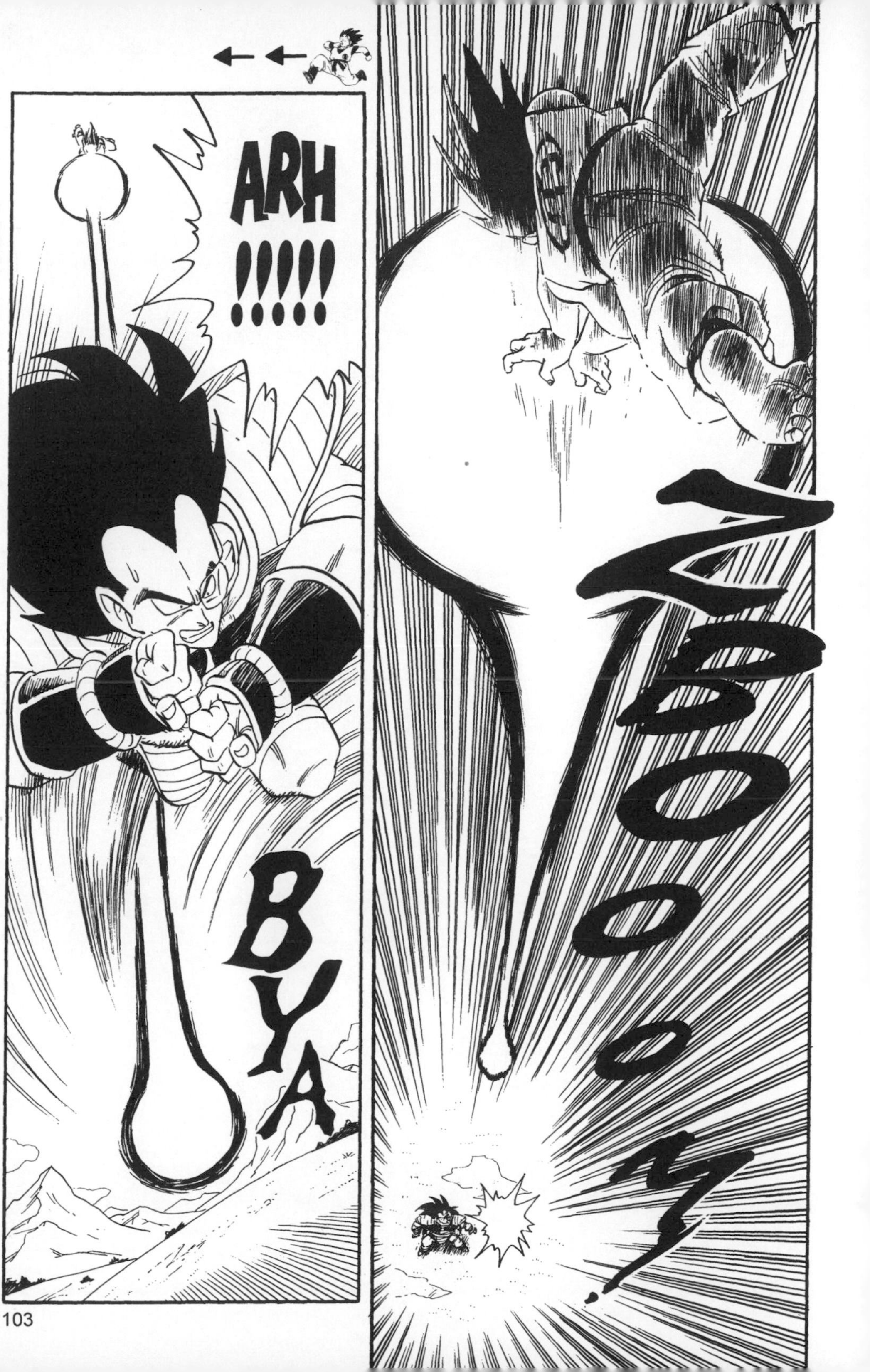

ZBOOOM!
ARH!!!!!
BYA

GWIII
GNNN

HWOOO

YOU... DARE ?!!
KI!

SHA

NNNNNN...

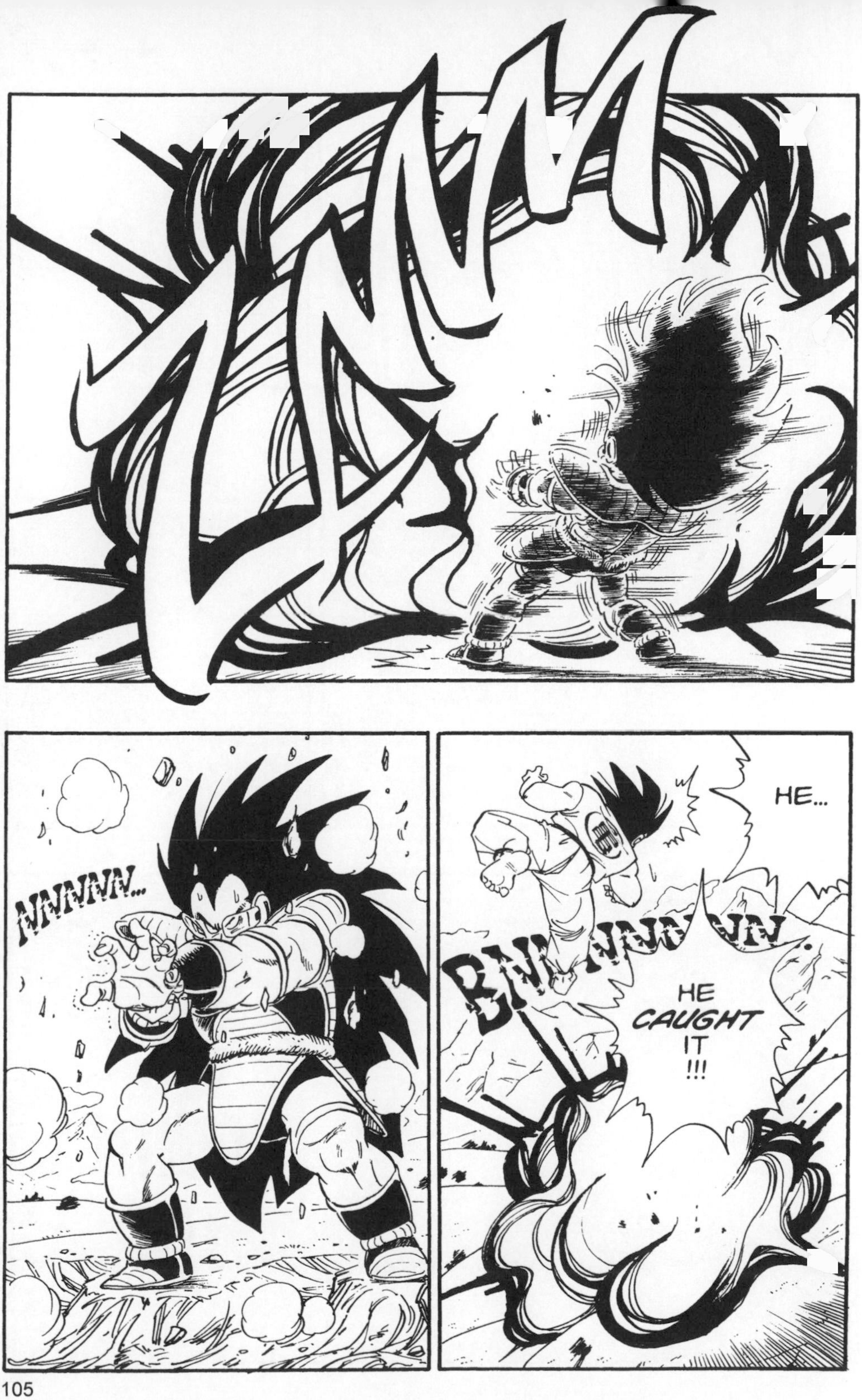

HE...
HE CAUGHT IT !!!

WHAT... IS HE MADE OF... ?

TRY THIS !!!

GUHH !!!!

SHHH

MM

DIE!!!
NKH... !!!

SOME-ONE... WILL DIE THIS DAY...!!!

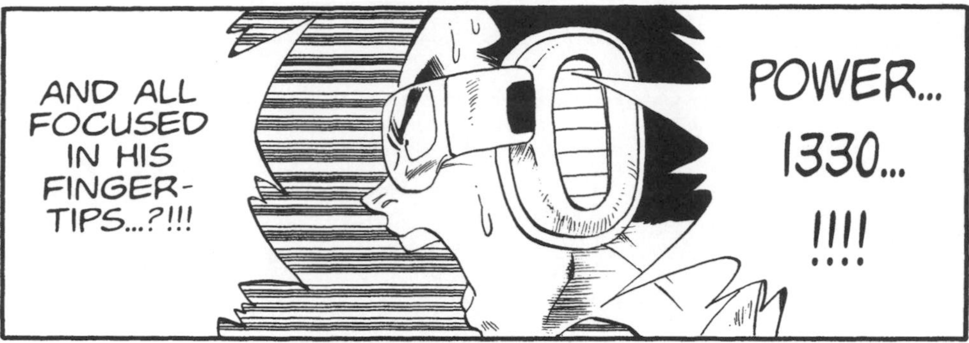
POWER... 1330... !!!!
AND ALL FOCUSED IN HIS FINGER-TIPS...?!!!

HOW ?!!!
HOW DO THEY DO IT ?!!!

ZHOOOM

DBZ:08 • A Surprise Appearance

ZHOOOM

GYURRRRR...!!

UH
!!!!
KRAK

...

HE...HE SIDE-STEPPED IT...!!
BUT NO ONE...CAN MOVE SO QUICKLY...

RIGHT THROUGH MY ARMOR... QUITE A BLAST...
IMAGINE IF I'D LET IT HIT ME...TSK... WOULDN'T BE MUCH LEFT OF ME, EH...?

THAT...
THAT WAS... MY LAST HOPE...

DO YOU SEE NOW, LITTLE BOYS...?
OUR PLAY TIME...IS OVER.

BY THE GODS...IS THIS THE END OF PICCOLO?

—IN ONE BLAST!

SHA

FARE-
WELL
!!!
HWOO

!!

YOU GOT... CARELESS...

...AND I GOT... YOUR TAIL...!

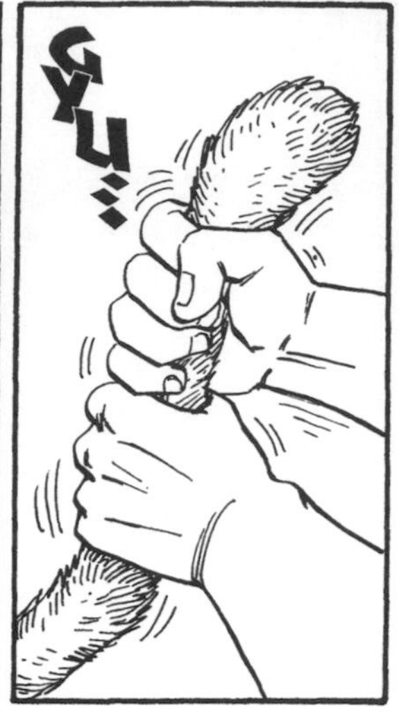
GYU...

WMP...
YOU... YOU'LL NEVER...

PICCOLO !!!
DO THAT THING AGAIN... *HURRY* !!!
WHAT...
OH... YES... !

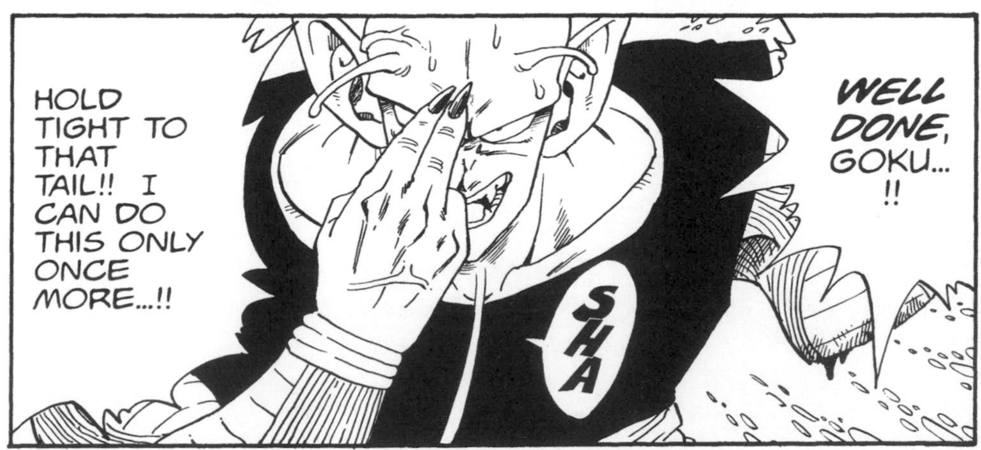
WELL DONE, GOKU... !!
SHA
HOLD TIGHT TO THAT TAIL!! I CAN DO THIS ONLY ONCE MORE...!!

K-KAKARROT... SURELY YOU WOULDN'T...KILL YOUR OWN BROTHER...

I TOLD YOU BEFORE!! YOU'RE NO BROTHER OF MINE!!
AND WHO TRIED TO KILL WHO FIRST, HUH ?!

YOU DIDN'T... TAKE ME *SERIOUSLY*...? I WAS ONLY... BLUFFING...!
LET ME GO... AND I'LL LEAVE THIS WORLD...

CLOSE YOUR EARS TO HIM, SON GOKU!!!
WHATEVER HE SAYS, HOLD THAT GRIP!!

PLEASE... LITTLE BROTHER... I KNOW I'VE DONE SOME TERRIBLE THINGS...
...
BUT PLEASE... LET ME LIVE...

ALL LIES !!!
HOLD HIM !!!

PLEASE, KAKARROT... !!
I SWEAR TO YOU !!

...

WOK

BNG

GMM
HNH !!

HEH!

NO !!
YOU... FOOL... !!!

WHAT A TREAT!! SUCH IDIOCY IS ALL TOO RARE!
HOW COULD I HAVE THOUGHT YOU COULD BE A WARRIOR ?
YOU... SCUM...

THE TRUE WARRIOR NEVER HESITATES TO KILL...
...NOT EVEN TO KILL HIS OWN BROTHER !
CARE FOR A DEMON-STRA-TION?

HERE!
GNN

KRAK
!!

NNNG-YAAA!!!!

AAH...
AAH...

NO HURRY, BROTHER. SUFFER MORE!

NNGH...!
AAA...!
GYARRH!!!

BE PATIENT! YOU'LL GET YOUR TURN!!
WHY NOT TAKE A SHOT AT ME IN THE MEANTIME, EH?!

BECAUSE... YOU WILL ONLY... DODGE IT AGAIN...

N-- NOOO--
NNNN... NYAAA!!!

BOOM

DBZ:09 • Goku's Last Chance...

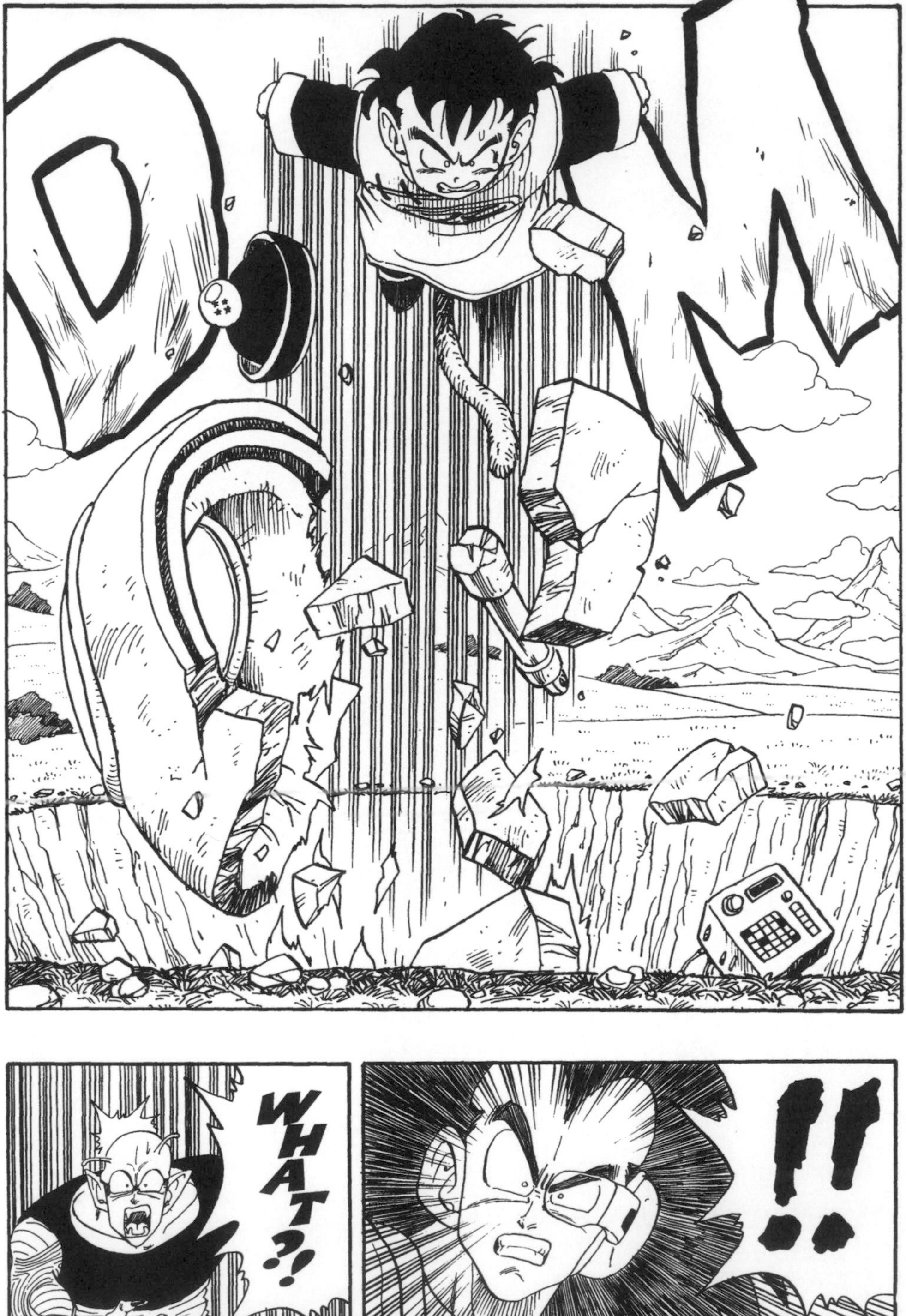

DOM

TUMP
!!

NNH
NNH
NNH

S-SON GOKU'S BOY... !!

GUH... G-GOHAN...?!
WHAT... IN THE... ?!

Y...
YOU... !

YOU... HURT MY...

...DADDYYYY!!!

WAAAH!!!!

BOOM

OOH
!!!!
....

NKH...!!!

DMF
OW
!!

?!

.....
.....
G...
GOHAN...

AA
!
DADDY...
DADDY...
!!
GOHAN...
RUN...

YOU...
DIRTY... LITTLE...

SOBB
RUN AWAY... NOW!!

YOUR POWER LEVEL... IT'S DROPPED TO 1!
IT CHANGES WITH YOUR EMOTIONS... DOESN'T IT?

BSSH!

DGG

STOP... IT...!!
H-HE'S... HE'S... ONLY...

"ONLY A CHILD"?! YOU'RE JOKING!
THE BRAT HAS MORE POWER THAN YOU!
PITY THAT HE'LL NEVER LEARN TO USE IT!

OH, DON'T WORRY... YOU'LL BE WITH HIM SOON...
...IN THE AFTERLIFE !

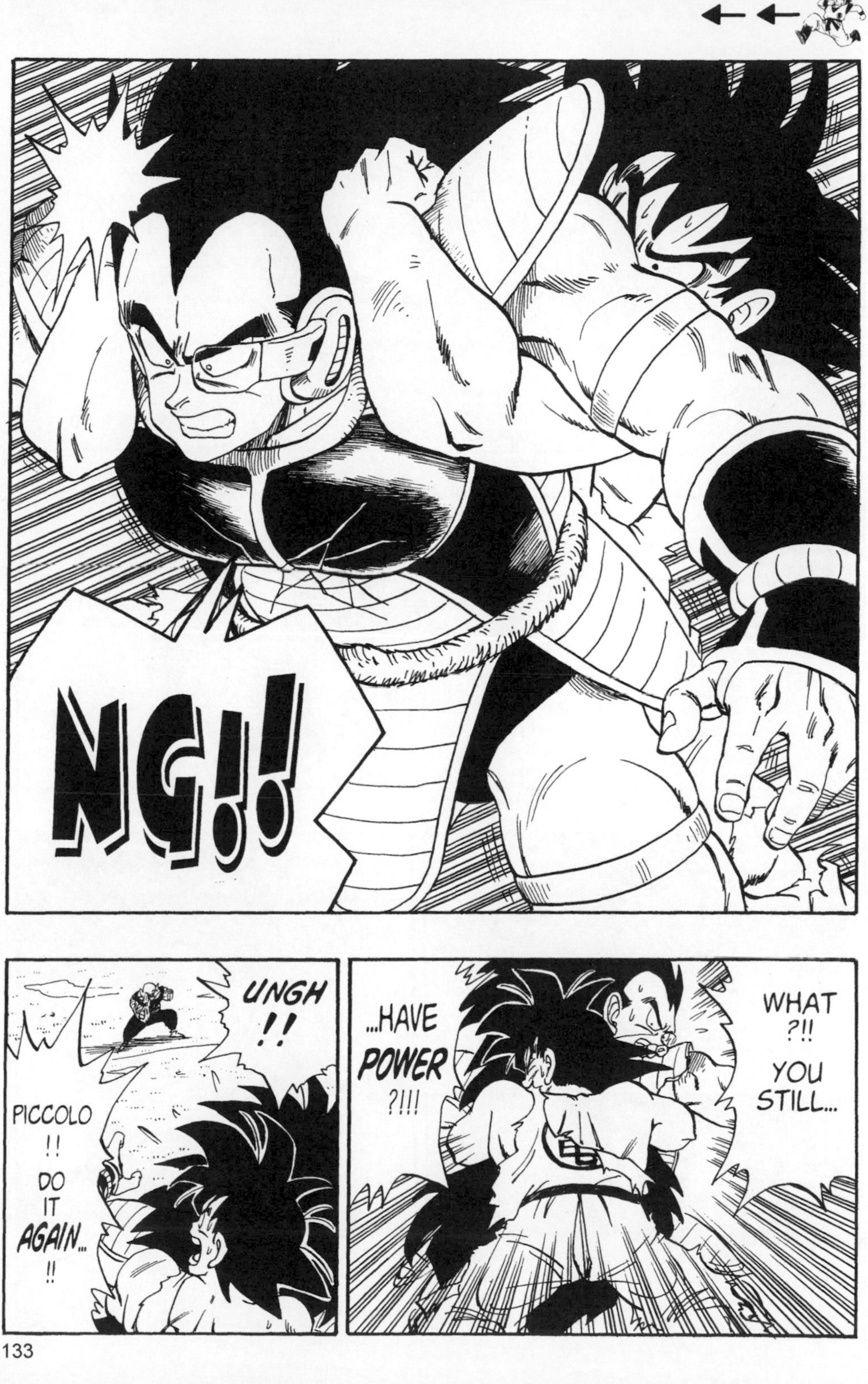

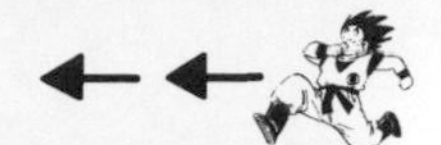

NG!!

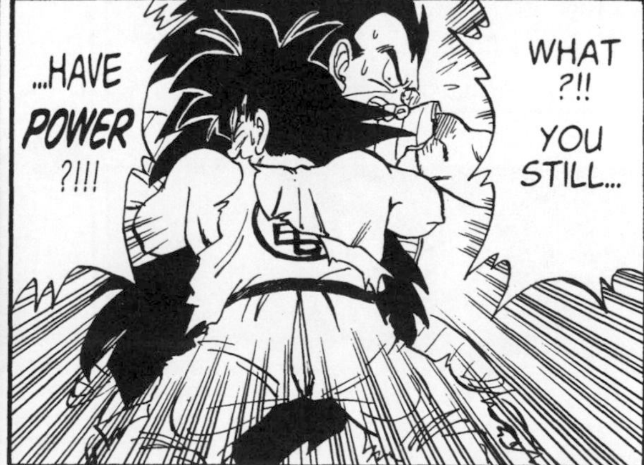

WHAT ?!! YOU STILL...
...HAVE POWER ?!!!

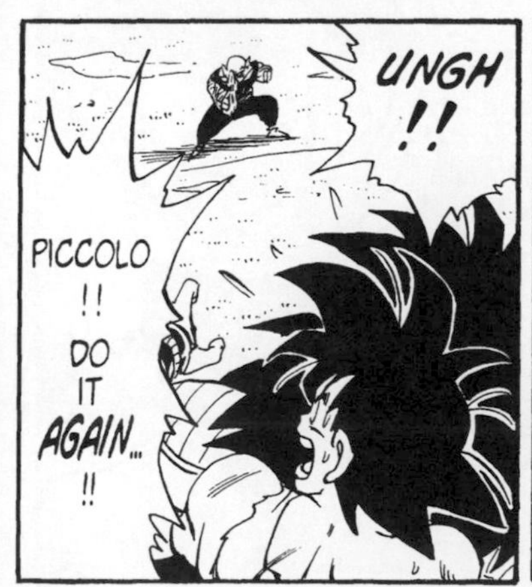

UNGH !!
PICCOLO !! DO IT AGAIN... !!

I AM BUILDING TO IT!!!
BUT I NEED TIME!!! WHY DID YOU NOT SEIZE HIS TAIL ?!!

'CAUSE... HE CAN... CUT HIS TAIL... OFF...!!
YOU... YOU KNOW... ?!

N... NKH !!
HURRY UP, WILL YOU ?!!

C...CURSE THE WHELP...!!
THAT STRIKE OF HIS... LEFT ME WEAKENED... !!!

LET ME GO, LITTLE BROTHER !!!
YOU'LL DIE TOO, IF HE KILLS ME!!!

HEH... IT'LL BE WORTH THE TRADE-OFF...!!

WH-WHAT DID YOU SAY?! YOU'RE INSANE...!!
IF IT'S THE ONLY WAY...TO DEFEAT YOU...!

SON GOKU...
I SHALL NOT HESITATE.
TO KILL YOU ALONG WITH HIM IS ONLY A BONUS FOR ME!

OF COURSE...IF YOUR FRIENDS STILL HAVE THEIR DRAGON BALLS...

AREN'T YOU... READY YET...?! M-MY RIBS... ARE BROKEN... !!
D-DO IT... NOW... !!

LET ME GO, KAKARROT!! I'LL LEAVE HERE FOREVER!!

Y-YOU WON'T...
FOOL ME TWICE...!!

LIGHT OF DEATH!!!!!

CURSE... YOU... !!!!

...HEH...!

DNSH

ZNNN

H-HOW...RIDICULOUS... THAT THE GREATNESS OF RADITZ... SHOULD END IN THE DUST...OF THIS... STUPID...LITTLE... WORLD...

HUFF... HUFF...
T-TAKE... THAT... !

HEH... HEH HEH...
GOT TO HAND IT...TO MY LITTLE BROTHER... WILLING TO DIE LIKE THAT...

FOOL. SON GOKU WILL NOT BE DEAD FOR LONG.
HE... WHAT... ?!

THE SEVEN DRAGON BALLS, MY FRIEND...
THEY CAN GRANT ANY WISH. THEY CAN EVEN BRING THE DEAD BACK TO LIFE.

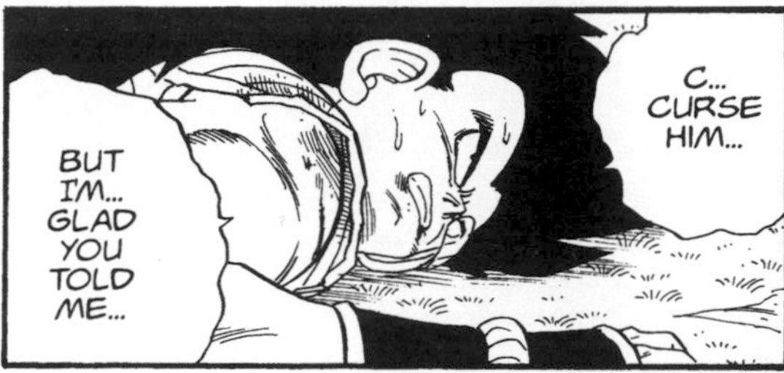
C... CURSE HIM...
BUT I'M... GLAD YOU TOLD ME...

...BECAUSE I'VE JUST...TRANSMITTED THE INFORMATION TO MY TWO PARTNERS IN THE DEPTHS OF SPACE... *HEHH*...
THEY KNOW... THAT I HAVE BEEN DEFEATED... AND THEY WILL... *COME* HERE...

...TO SWEEP THIS PLANET CLEAN OF ALL ITS... HUMAN VERMIN... INCLUDING YOU...
...AND THEN... NO DOUBT... THEY'LL BRING ME BACK TO LIFE...

...

WH-
WHEN...
ARE THEY...
...G-GOING TO GET... HERE...
IN YOUR TERMS... ONE YEAR... HEHH...

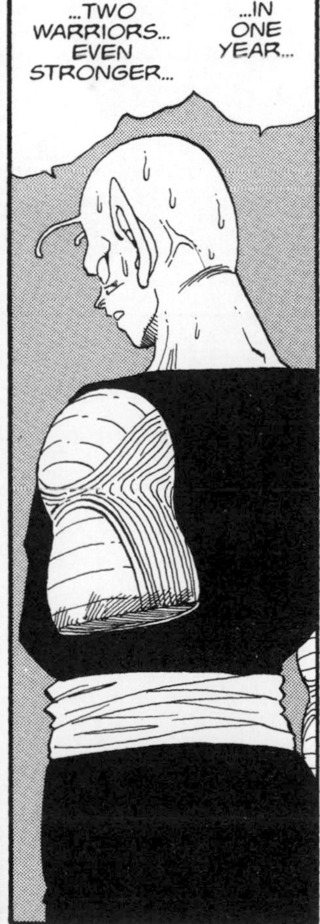
...IN ONE YEAR...
...TWO WARRIORS... EVEN STRONGER...

AND HOW DO YOU... LIKE YOUR ODDS...EH... ?
I HOPE YOU... ENJOY YOUR... LAST YEAR... HEHH... HEHH...

...

TR... TRANSIENT JOYS... ARE THE SWEETEST...
JUST ASK... YOUR FELLOW INSECTS...

GAAAH!!!!!!

DM

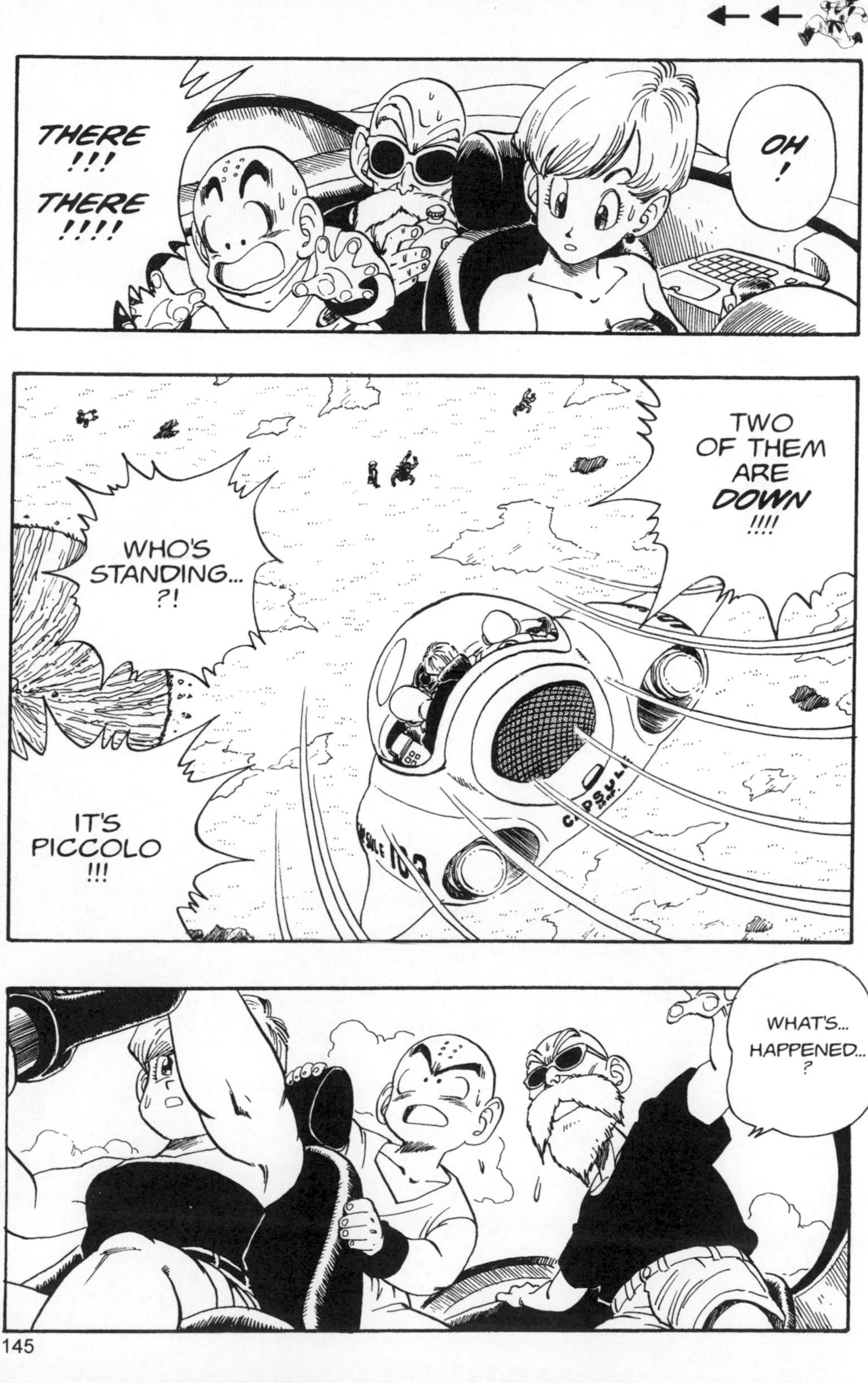

TWO OF THEM ARE DOWN!!!!

WHO'S STANDING...?!

IT'S PICCOLO!!!

MEANWHILE, IN DEEP SPACE...

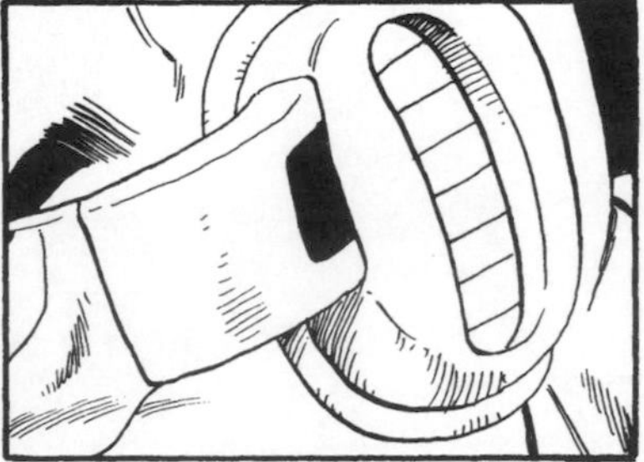

RADITZ...
...IS DEAD...

HE DESERVED IT...
KILLED BY POWER LEVELS BARELY OVER A THOUSAND...
WE CAN LEAVE THIS PLANET FOR LATER...

HOW ABOUT IMMORTALITY FOR OURSELVES? NO DEATH! NO AGE!

ONLY AN ETERNITY OF *COMBAT* !!

AH...! NOW *THAT'S* A WISH !!

THE POWER OF KAKARROT'S SON... IMPOSSIBLY HIGH FOR A SAIYAN CHILD...
MAYBE HIS READING WAS WRONG.

I DON'T THINK SO. NOT WITH THE AMOUNT OF DAMAGE RADITZ SUFFERED FROM THAT ONE STRIKE...
IT SEEMS THAT MIXING SAIYAN AND EARTHLING BLOOD BEGETS A POWERFUL HYBRID...

A SUPER SAIYAN, EH... ?
SO IF WE SPAWN A FLOCK OF THEM OURSELVES...
...WE COULD BUILD ANOTHER SAIYAN EMPIRE!

DON'T BE STUPID.
DO YOU WANT A LOT OF INGRATE BRATS RUNNING AROUND WITH POWERS GREATER THAN ***OURS***?

OH... RIGHT...
WE MUST EXTERMINATE ALL LIFE ON EARTH!

YOU... YOU MEAN...
I DO INDEED...
GOKU! HEY, GOKU!
DON'T GIVE UP! HANG ON!!

GOHAN'S ALL RIGHT.
JUST KNOCKED OUT...

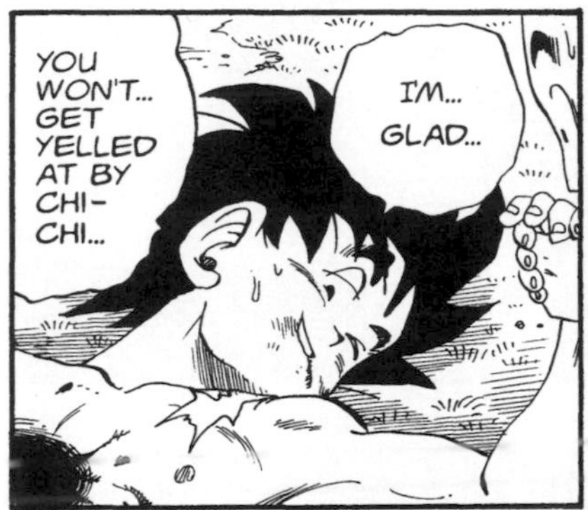
I'M... GLAD...
YOU WON'T... GET YELLED AT BY CHI-CHI...

KURI... RIN... DYING'S NOT... MUCH FUN... IS IT...?
D-DON'T TALK LIKE THAT... WE'LL BRING YOU BACK...!

HEH... THANKS...
HAHH!

...
...GOKU...?

WAA!!!
FFT
HE VANISHED!!!!

I SENSE...
...THAT CURSED KAMI-SAMA'S HAND IN THIS.

HUH?!
WHO ELSE COULD DO SUCH A THING?
HE MUST HAVE PLANS FOR SON GOKU AGAIN... QUEER ONES, NO DOUBT...

NOW, THEN... TIME FOR A LONG SLEEP.
I CAN'T WAIT...TO WAKE UP!

DragonBallZ

VOLUME 2

THE LORD OF WORLDS

DBZ:11 • A Warrior in Hell

WHAT...?! KAMI-SAMA TOOK GOKU'S **BODY**...?!
WH-WHO KNOWS WHAT HE'LL DO...
BUT IF IT'S THE DIVINE **KAMI-SAMA,** WE DON'T HAVE TO WORRY, RIGHT? R-RIGHT...?

WE'VE JUST GOTTA GATHER THE OTHER SIX DRAGON BALLS...
...TO BRING GOKU BACK TO LIFE.
ARRGH! WHERE DID YAMCHA GO, NOW THAT WE NEED HIM ?!
DIDN'T **YOU** CHASE HIM AWAY...?

?!
WAIT A MINUTE... THAT SO-CALLED BROTHER OF GOKU'S...
HOW'D HE **FIND** HIM SO EASILY...?

THE QUEER MACHINE MOUNTED ON HIS FACE SEEMS TO TRACK AN OPPONENT'S STRENGTH AND POSITION...
HUH ?

Y... Y'MEAN... THAT...?
Y-YOU GO GET IT, OKAY, KURIRIN...?
...
UH... RIGHT. BUT... HE WON'T COME BACK TO LIFE, WILL HE...?

KLAK KLAK
PIPIII
WOW... !

HMM...
GOT IT... GOT IT...
THIS DOES THAT, AND *THAT*...

THIS IS ONE AWE-SOME MACHINE!
A LITTLE BANGED UP, BUT I SHOULD BE ABLE TO FIX IT.
YOU'RE MY HERO, Y'KNOW THAT?

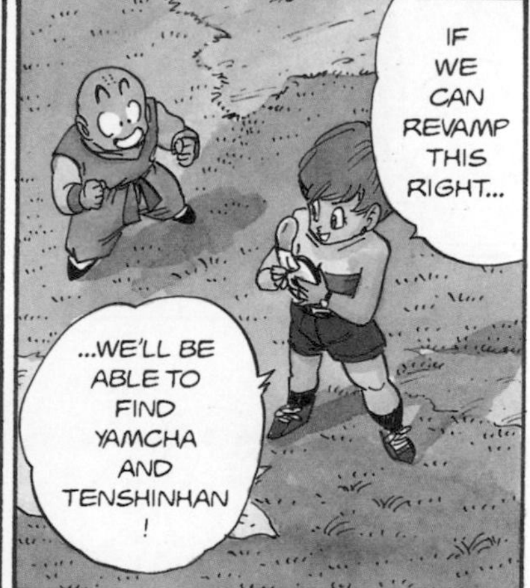
IF WE CAN REVAMP THIS RIGHT...
...WE'LL BE ABLE TO FIND YAMCHA AND TENSHINHAN !

THEN LET'S HURRY BACK TO THE TURTLE HOUSE.*
YEAH... WE CAN'T DO ANYTHING HERE.
AND THEN I'LL HEAD RIGHT OUT AFTER THOSE DRAGON BALLS!

*THE "TURTLE HOUSE"... ALSO KNOWN AS THE "KAME HOUSE"–ED.

NNNGG..!!!

PICCOLO... WHAT ARE YOU GOING TO-

WHEW
TWIK TWIK

..GGYAAA!!!
ZHOOP

...
UH...
L-LIKE A... LIZARD...

BE SURE TO FIND THOSE DRAGON BALLS. EVEN KAMI-SAMA LACKS THE POWER TO BRING THE DEAD BACK TO LIFE.
IN THE MEANTIME... *I'll* TAKE GOKU'S SON.

WH-WHAT?!
Y-YOU'RE KIDDING! WH-WHAT ARE YOU GONNA...

I *KNOW*!
YOU'RE GONNA *EAT* HIM!!
I AM *NOT*!!!

THAT BOY WILL BE A POWERFUL ASSET... ONCE HE'S TRAINED.
WE'LL NEED HIS POWER AGAINST THE TWO SAIYANS WHO WILL BE HERE WITHIN THE YEAR...
...AND ONLY *I* CAN TRAIN HIM PROPERLY.

W-W-WELL YEAH, B-BUT...
IT'S KIND OF A BIG RESPONSI-BILITY, RIGHT...?
W- WE SHOULD ASK GOKU OR CHI-CHI BEFORE WE—
WE HAVE NO TIME FOR THAT!
TRY TO STOP ME AND I'LL KILL YOU ALL!

IN ONE YEAR'S TIME, I'LL BRING THE BRAT BACK TO YOU.
TELL SON GOKU TO BE PATIENT... IF HE COMES BACK TO LIFE, THAT IS.

HYUUUU
B-BUT... BUT...!

...
D-D-DON'T LOOK AT ME...!!
IF THE KID'S LUCKY... HE'LL ONLY TURN INTO A SUPER-VILLAIN...

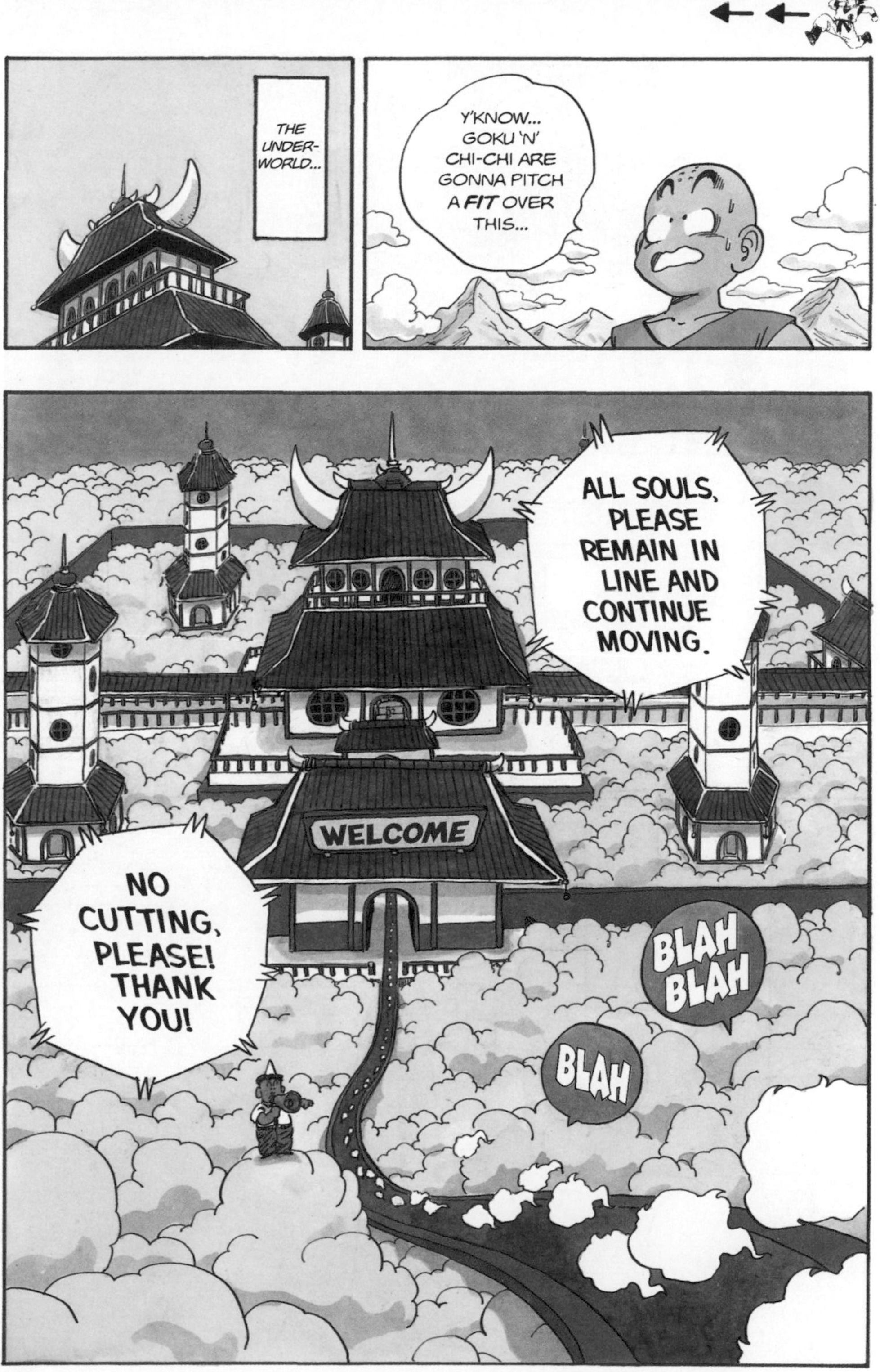

Y'KNOW... GOKU 'N' CHI-CHI ARE GONNA PITCH A **FIT** OVER THIS...

THE UNDER-WORLD...

ALL SOULS, PLEASE REMAIN IN LINE AND CONTINUE MOVING.

WELCOME

NO CUTTING, PLEASE! THANK YOU!

BLAH BLAH

BLAH

...AND SO HE HAS COME, STILL IN FLESH FORM, TO RECEIVE TRAINING.
DOES HE HAVE YOUR PERMISSION TO PROCEED TO KAIŌ-SAMA, LORD ENMA?*

LET ME SEE... SON GOKU... QUITE A LIST OF MERITORIOUS ACHIEVEMENTS HERE...

ENOUGH TO FLY STRAIGHT TO THE ***UPPER*** WORLD, IN FACT... AND YET YOU WANT HIM TO RISK THE SERPENT ROAD TO SEE THE LORD OF WORLDS?

THE HON. ENMA

YES SIR.

*ENMA DAI-O, KNOWN IN JAPANESE MYTH AND FOLKLORE AS THE LORD AND JUDGE OF THE DEAD!

SAY, DOES EVERYONE COME HERE WHEN THEY DIE?
THEY DO.
EVEN ALIENS?
YOU'RE HERE, AREN'T YOU? THE DEAD OF *ALL* WORLDS COME HERE FOR RELOCATION, EITHER TO HEAVEN OR HELL...

HEY, DID A GUY NAMED *RADITZ* COME HERE A LITTLE WHILE AGO?
EH?
AK! DON'T SPEAK TO A LORD LIKE THAT!
THE HON. ENMA

YES, HE DID. YOUR BROTHER, WASN'T HE? STRAIGHT TO HELL, OF COURSE.
WHO'S WHO

DIDN'T HE FIGHT IT?!

INDEED HE DID. BUT NONE DEFEAT ME.
WHOA...!
CLOSED

BEATING *THAT* GUY...
NOW *THAT'S* AWE-SOME!

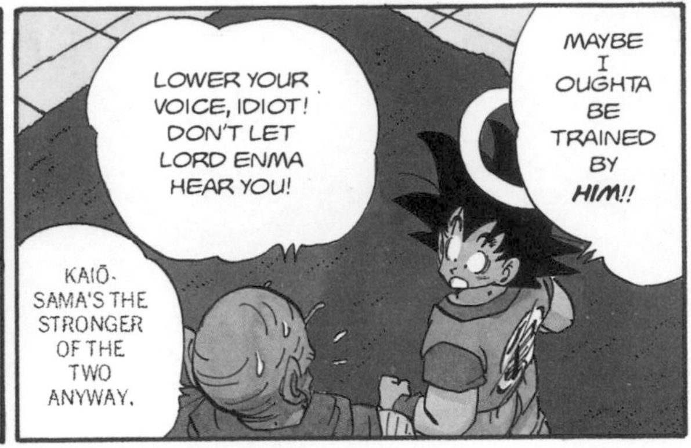

MAYBE I OUGHTA BE TRAINED BY *HIM!!*
KAIŌ-SAMA'S THE STRONGER OF THE TWO ANYWAY.
LOWER YOUR VOICE, IDIOT! DON'T LET LORD ENMA HEAR YOU!

I HEARD THAT.
PERHAPS KAMI-SAMA NEEDS A LITTLE RE-TRAINING IN HELL, *HMM?*

F-F-FORGIVE ME, MY LORD! I DIDN'T THINK YOU'D HEAR...
I-I MEAN... WHAT BIG EARS YOU HAVE... *HA HA...*
...
YOU NEVER WERE A VERY FUNNY GOD...
THE HON. ENMA

IT IS DONE!
IF YOU WANT THE LORD OF WORLDS SO BADLY... GO!

WAIT FOR THE GUIDE BY THE SIDE ENTRANCE.
TH-TH-THANK YOU, SIR!
THE HON. ENMA
PLEASE NOTE MANAGEMENT TAKES NO RESPONSIBILITY FOR WHAT HAPPENS ON THE SERPENT ROAD.

WELL, THEN... GOOD LUCK. YOU'LL NEED IT THIS YEAR.
I'LL TAKE YOUR WORD FOR IT! I'LL TELL KAIŌ-SAMA, THIS "LORD OF WORLDS" GUY, THAT YOU SENT ME!
SAY HI TO MR. POPO FOR ME, HUH?

WHAT A FINE MESS THE EARTH HAS GOTTEN ITSELF INTO...
THIS TIME, WE MAY NOT COME THROUGH SO EASILY...

TRUE, WE COULD VERY WELL ASK SHENLONG FOR THE OBLITERATION OF THE SAIYANS, BUT EVEN **HIS** POWER MAY NOT BE ENOUGH...
SON GOKU MAY BE TRAINED BY THE LORD OF WORLDS, BUT WE CANNOT KNOW HOW MUCH STRONGER HE CAN BECOME...
MMBLE...
OUR ONLY HOPE MAY LIE WITH GOKU'S SON... AND HOW DO WE KNOW WHAT PICCOLO WILL RAISE HIM TO BE...?

MTTER...

SHUT UP !!!
WILL YOU QUIT **THINKING** SO LOUD?!
YOW !!!
THE HON. ENMA

SORRY TO KEEP YOU WAITING! I'LL BE YOUR GUIDE TO THE HEAD OF THE SERPENT. IT'S QUITE A TRIP! ARE YOU IN GOOD HEALTH?
PUTT PUTT PUTT
ASIDE FROM BEING **DEAD,** YOU MEAN...?

...SAY, WHAT'S THIS "LORD OF WORLDS" LIKE?
WHO, KAIŌ-SAMA? THE LORD OF WORLDS STANDS ABOVE ALL THE GODS OF THE UNIVERSE!

BINGO!
HERE WE ARE!

Y-YOU MEAN THE "SERPENT ROAD" IS REALLY A ***SERPENT***?! N-NOW WHAT?!
FOLLOW THE GREEN SCALE ROAD! IT'LL LEAD YOU STRAIGHT TO THE LORD HIMSELF!

H-HOW LONG IS IT...?
LEGEND SAYS IT'S ABOUT A MILLION KILOMETERS.

A MUH... MUH...
HAS ANYBODY EVER REACHED THE *END*?!

ABSOLUTELY! LORD ENMA'S DONE IT! AND IN JUST THE PAST HUNDRED MILLION YEARS!

AND N-NOBODY ELSE...?
WELL... IF ONE GUY CAN DO IT... TWO GUYS CAN DO DO IT...

BE CAREFUL NOT TO FALL OFF INTO THE CLOUDS.
HELL'S RIGHT DOWN THERE, AND YOU'LL NEVER GET OUT.
R-RIGHT...

GEEZ... I DIDN'T EVEN BRING A LUNCH...
YOU'LL BE FINE, SIR! YOU'RE ALREADY DEAD, SO YOU CERTAINLY CAN'T STARVE TO DEATH!
OH YEAH...

ONE LAST FAVOR BEFORE I GO... DO YOU KNOW THE OLD FORTUNE-TELLER?*
OH, YES, SHE'S ALWAYS POPPING IN!

GREAT! NEXT TIME SHE COMES, CAN YOU TELL HER TO TELL KAME-SEN'NIN NOT TO BRING ME BACK TO LIFE FOR ONE YEAR?

NO TROUBLE!
"TURTLE HERMIT... ONE YEAR..." GOT IT!

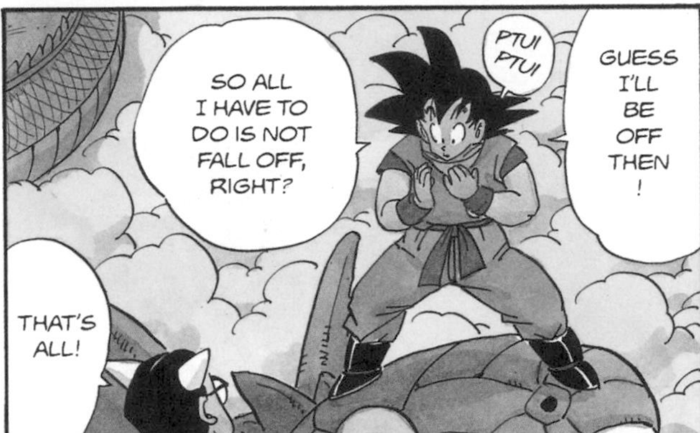

GUESS I'LL BE OFF THEN!
PTUI PTUI
SO ALL I HAVE TO DO IS NOT FALL OFF, RIGHT?
THAT'S ALL!

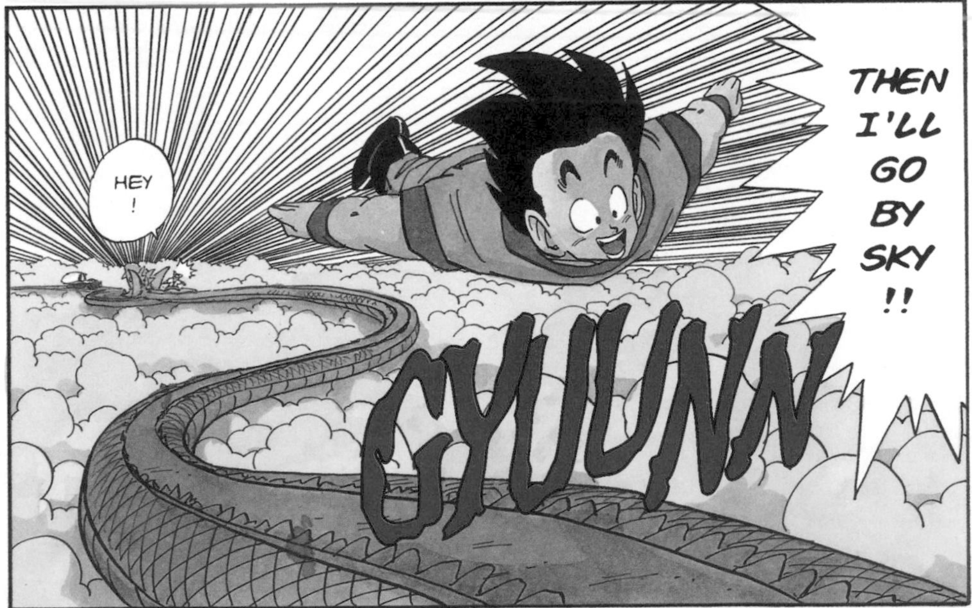

THEN I'LL GO BY SKY!!
HEY!
GYUUNN

*A.K.A. "BABA URANAI," A WISE OLD CRONE (LIKE BABA YAGA!) FIRST MET BY GOKU & CO. IN EARLIER **DRAGON BALL** STORIES.

THAT'S NOT FAIR...

VEEEEN

W-WE CAN'T KEEP THIS FROM CHI-CHI... KURIRIN, WHY DON'T YOU RUN OVER THERE AND TELL HER, *HMM...?*
WH-WH-WHY DO *I* HAVE TO?!
'CAUSE ***WE*** DON'T WANNA GET KILLED...

AUGH... BLAST IT...!
I USED UP TOO MUCH POWER IN FLIGHT...!

DBZ:12 • Gohan and Piccolo

FEH!

BLOOSH

BURBLE URBLE

HUHH !

KOFF
KOFF

huff huff
?!

WE HAVE TO TALK. GET OUT OF THE WATER.
HUH ?!

EEK!
WH-WHO ARE YOU...?!

!!!
WH-WHERE'S DADDY...?!

DAAA-DDY!!! WHERE ARE YOU?!
BLASH BLASH
HELP MEEEEE!!!

DAD-DYYYY! WAAAAH!!!
I'M SCARED!!!

MY BOY...
I THINK YOU'VE GIVEN ME...

...MORE THAN ENOUGH TROUBLE!
BLASH
BLASH
EEK!!!
AAA!!!

WAAAAH!!!
WAAAAH!!!

SILENCE!!!!
OR I'LL SLIT YOUR THROAT!!!

snff
snff
NOW LISTEN TO ME...

YOUR FATHER IS *DEAD*!
HE GAVE HIS LIFE TO SAVE YOU FROM THAT KIDNAPPER!

!!

D...
DAD-D-D-DY...

DON'T EVEN *START*, BOY!
snff
snff

YOU'VE HEARD ABOUT THE DRAGON BALLS, HAVEN'T YOU? GOKU'S FRIENDS WILL GATHER THEM AND HE WILL EVENTUALLY BE BROUGHT BACK TO LIFE.
HIS *DEATH* IS NOT THE PROBLEM.
WE DEFEATED YOUR KIDNAPPER... BUT TWO OTHERS EVEN MORE POWERFUL THAN HE ARE ON THEIR WAY HERE.

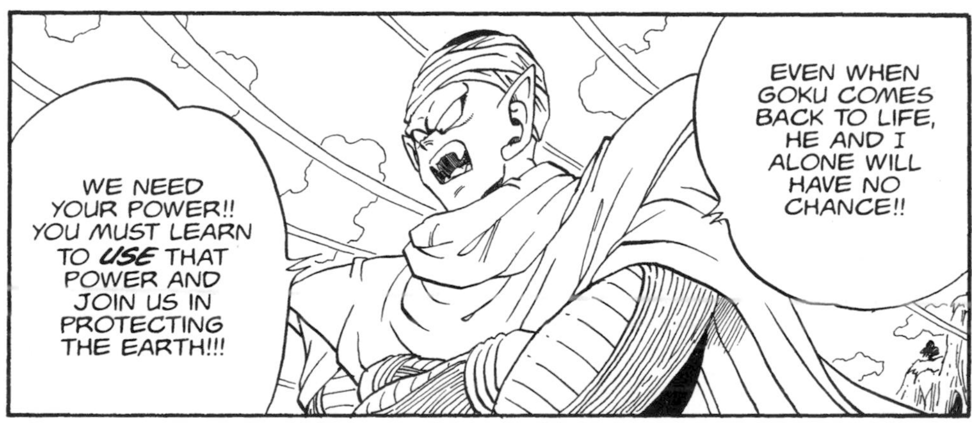

EVEN WHEN GOKU COMES BACK TO LIFE, HE AND I ALONE WILL HAVE NO CHANCE!!
WE NEED YOUR POWER!! YOU MUST LEARN TO *USE* THAT POWER AND JOIN US IN PROTECTING THE EARTH!!!

WHAT...?! MUH-MUH-MUH-*ME*?!
B-B-BUT I C-CAN'T FIGHT...I CAN'T!!

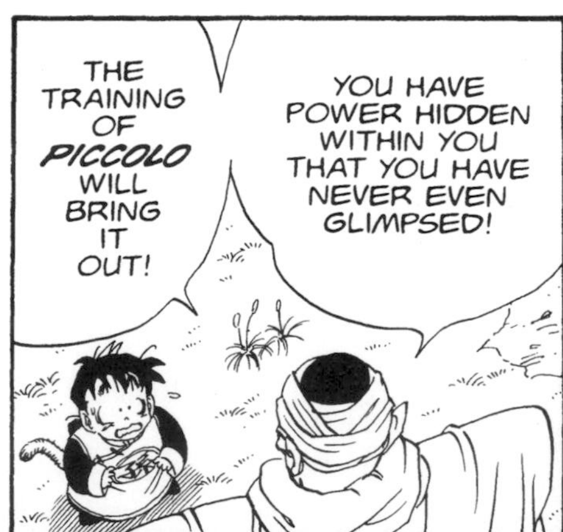

YOU HAVE POWER HIDDEN WITHIN YOU THAT YOU HAVE NEVER EVEN GLIMPSED!
THE TRAINING OF *PICCOLO* WILL BRING IT OUT!

Y-YOU'RE LYING...
I...I DON'T HAVE ANY POWER...

DO YOU WANT **PROOF** ?

GLOMP
NO !!
STOP !!

OWWW !!
WHAT ARE YOU **DOING** ?!

EEEEK !!!

AAAAA!!!

YAA!!
EEE-YAA!!

WAAA!!!

FIND THE POWER QUICKLY, BOY...

...OR TURN TO JELLY AGAINST THOSE ROCKS!!

ARH

VVMMM
GWOOM

ZZZH

HYUUUUUUU...

!!

THAT'S... MORE THAN I IMAGINED...

...

WHAT AM I IN FOR...?
REARING THE CUB WHO MAY SOMEDAY BECOME MY MOST FORMIDABLE FOE...?

D-DID I...DO THAT... ?!
IT BEGINS TO COME CLEAR, DOESN'T IT, BOY?

YOUR POWER BURSTS LOOSE ONLY WHEN YOUR EMOTIONS ARE AT THEIR PEAK...
...AND THEN ONLY FOR AN INSTANT. NOT VERY USEFUL...
BUT I WILL TEACH YOU HOW TO USE THAT POWER ALL THE TIME. I WILL MAKE YOU THE GREATEST FIGHTER EVER!

BUT... BUT I...
...I DON'T WANT TO BE A FIGHTER... I WANT TO BE A GREAT SCHOLAR...

BE WHATEVER YOU WANT, INFANT... AFTER YOU'VE DEFEATED THE TWO SAIYANS WHO WILL BE HERE NEXT YEAR.
IF YOU FAIL, THEY'LL EXTERMINATE EVERYONE ON EARTH. THAT WOULD PUT A CRIMP IN YOUR CAREER PLANS, EH?

B-BUT I'M...I'M SCARED...

QUIT WHINING!!! OR I'LL KILL YOU RIGHT NOW!!!
DISCUSSION TIME IS OVER!!! TAKE OFF YOUR SURCOAT!!!

LOOK AT THE WAY HE'S COSSETED YOU. HE DOESN'T HAVE THE ***TOUGHNESS*** THAT IS PLAINLY NEEDED...
TOO BAD. HE'S POWERFUL, BUT HE'S NO COMBAT-MASTER.

BUT IF...IF DADDY...
snff
...IF HE'S COMING BACK TO LIFE, I WANT TO BE TRAINED BY HIM.

A-CHOO!!

AND SO HE RUNS AND RUNS AND RUNS... LITTLE DREAMING OF HIS ONLY SON'S MISERY...

?

Sniff...

DBZ:13 • Son Gohan, the Inconsolable

WH-WHAT DO I DO... F-FOR TRAINING... ?

IF YOU'RE STILL ALIVE WHEN I COME BACK IN SIX MONTHS...
...I'LL TEACH YOU HOW TO FIGHT.

A-ALONE FOR SIX MONTHS AT A PLACE LIKE THIS...?!
I-I DON'T WANT TO, I-I'LL DIE OF LONELI-NESS!!

LISTEN! YOU HAVE NO TIME FOR THIS INFANTILE BEHAVIOR!
SURVIVE FOR SIX MONTHS SOMEHOW, AND LEARN HOW TO BE TOUGH.
MENTALLY *AND* PHYSICALLY!

DON'T FORGET THAT YOU HOLD THE KEY TO THE EARTH'S FATE.
BELIEVE IN YOUR POWER. AND FIGURE OUT BY YOURSELF HOW TO EFFECTIVELY DRAW OUT THAT POWER.
B-BUT BUT I...!

HEH HEH...YOU WON'T BE ALONE. THIS PLACE IS SWARMING WITH BLOOD-THIRSTY BEASTS.
WH-WHAT?! D-DON'T, PLEASE DON'T LEAVE ME!!

SEE YA.
OH, AND BY THE WAY–DON'T EVEN THINK ABOUT ESCAPING. THIS PLACE IS SURROUNDED BY DESERT...
A WORLD OF DEATH THAT MAKES THIS PLACE LOOK LIKE A PARADISE.

W-WAIT!
WHERE DO I GET FOOD?!
AND A BATH?! AND A BED?!

DO YOU THINK THOSE THINGS ARE PREPARED FOR YOU?
POOR LITTLE PRINCE-LING...

...
B-BUT... THAT'S NOT FAIR...

IF YOU WANT TO FEEL RESENTMENT, CURSE YOUR OWN FATE... AS DO I.

VOO

AH !!!

...

YOU SEEM TROUBLED, MY LORD...
WHAT IS THE MATTER?

OUR PICCOLO... IT SEEMS THAT HE IS INDEED DIFFERENT FROM BEFORE...
HE IS DEFINITELY EVIL, BUT IT FEELS LIKE THE CRUDE, CUNNING VIOLENCE HE ONCE HAD IS GONE...
THAT WAS MY THOUGHT AS WELL... ONE THING IS CERTAIN—NO LONGER IS HE THE "DAI-MAŌ" OF OLD.

I KNEW THAT THERE WAS SOMETHING AMISS WHEN RADITZ'S SOUL, AFTER HE WAS KILLED BY PICCOLO, ENDED UP IN THE UNDERWORLD...
USUALLY, THE SOULS OF THOSE KILLED BY DEMONS CANNOT REST IN PEACE AND DRIFT IN SPACE, SUFFERING... THE FACT THAT RADITZ IS IN THE UNDERWORLD MEANS THAT PICCOLO IS CLEARLY DIFFERENT FROM BEFORE...

PERHAPS HE IS EVEN AWARE OF IT...
...AWARE THAT I... AND THUS HE, PICCOLO... HAVE ONLY ONE YEAR TO LIVE...

...
ONE YEAR...

I DO NOT KNOW, HOWEVER, IF THAT IS BECAUSE PICCOLO IS GOING TO BE KILLED BY THE SAIYANS WHEN THEY ARRIVE IN A YEAR...
...OR BECAUSE MY LIFE SPAN HAPPENS TO END AT THAT TIME...

MY DEATH IS PICCOLO'S DEATH, AND PICCOLO'S DEATH IS MY DEATH...
HEH HEH... IT IS NOT A PLEASANT THING, EVEN AS A GOD, TO KNOW ONE'S OWN DEATH...

HE KNOWS THIS...
HE MIGHT BE WANTING TO LEAVE SOMETHING BEHIND... EVEN IF IT IS IN SON GOKU'S SON...

THEN THE DRAGON BALLS...
YES...THE NEXT TIME THEY ARE USED WILL BE THEIR LAST...

WEHH...
I'M SCAAARED...
sob sob...

BOOM BOOM

BOOM
SNIFF...

!!

GRRR...
A...
W...
WHA...
OHH OHH OHH
GRAUGH

WAAH!

STOMP

STOMP

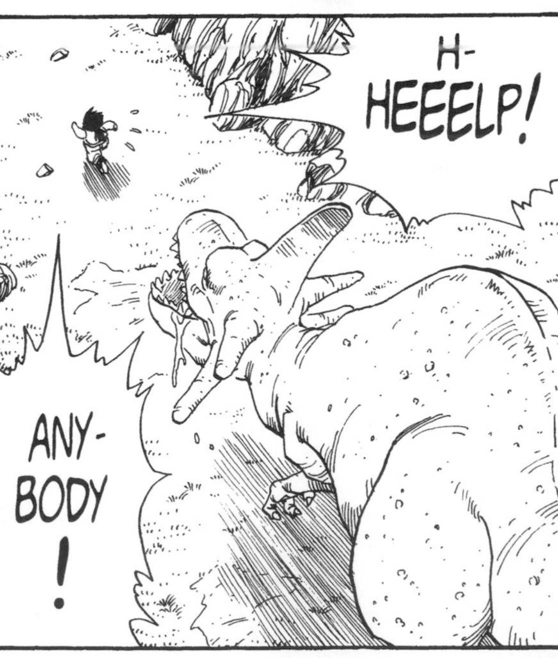

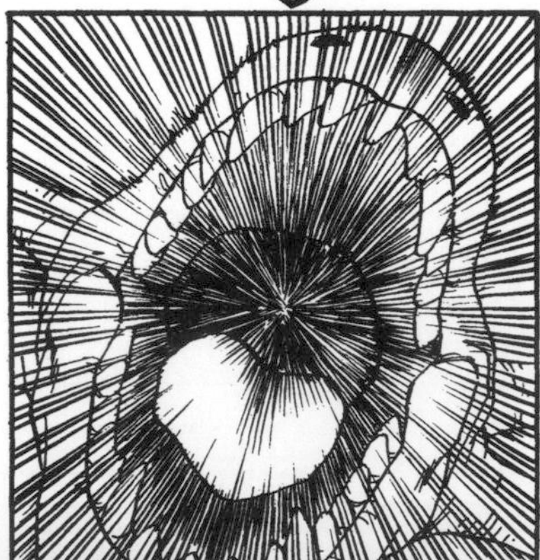

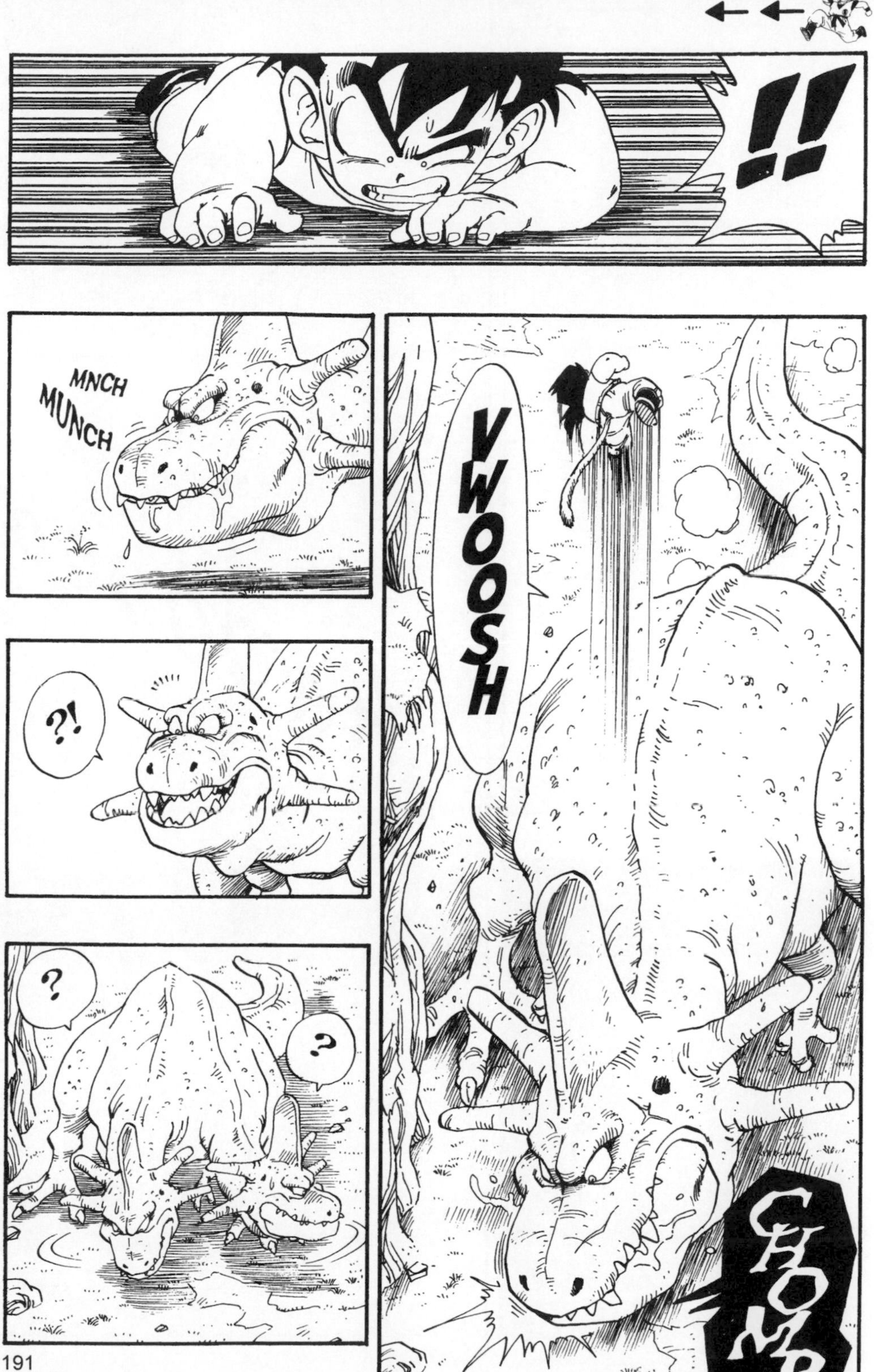

!!

VWOOSH
CHOMP

MNCH
MUNCH

?!

?
?

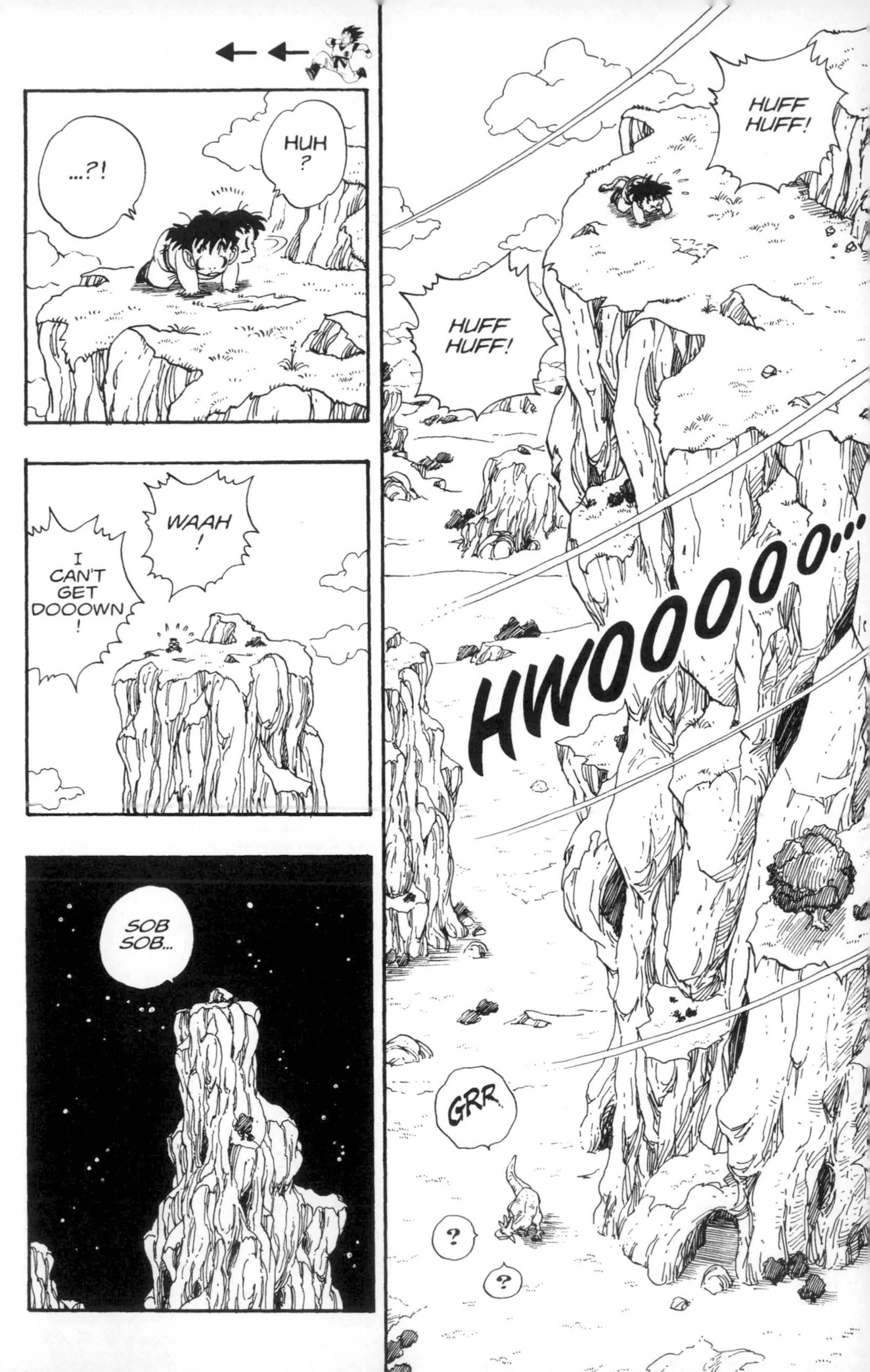
HUFF HUFF!
HUFF HUFF!
HWOOOOOO...
GRR
?
?
HUH ?
...?!
WAAH !
I CAN'T GET DOOOWN !
SOB SOB...

I'M SCAAARED...
I'M HUNGRYYY...

RMBL
I'M STAARVIIING...
I'M GONNA DIE...

?!

OH !!

APPLES !!
THERE'S APPLES HERE !!
YAAY!

!

?
?

I WANNA EAT DIM-SUM...

MNCH MUNCH MNCH

BUT KNOW YOU WELL— THIS IS THE **LAST** TIME...
IF YOU CANNOT SURVIVE ON YOUR OWN AFTER THIS, IT ONLY CONFIRMS THAT YOUR USES ARE AS LIMITED AS I FIRST THOUGHT.
Z...
Z...

HUFF
HUFF

VWOO

SWIP SWIP SWIP

ARG!
I'M SO **HUNGRY**!

DBZ:14 · Deeds Done by the Full Moon

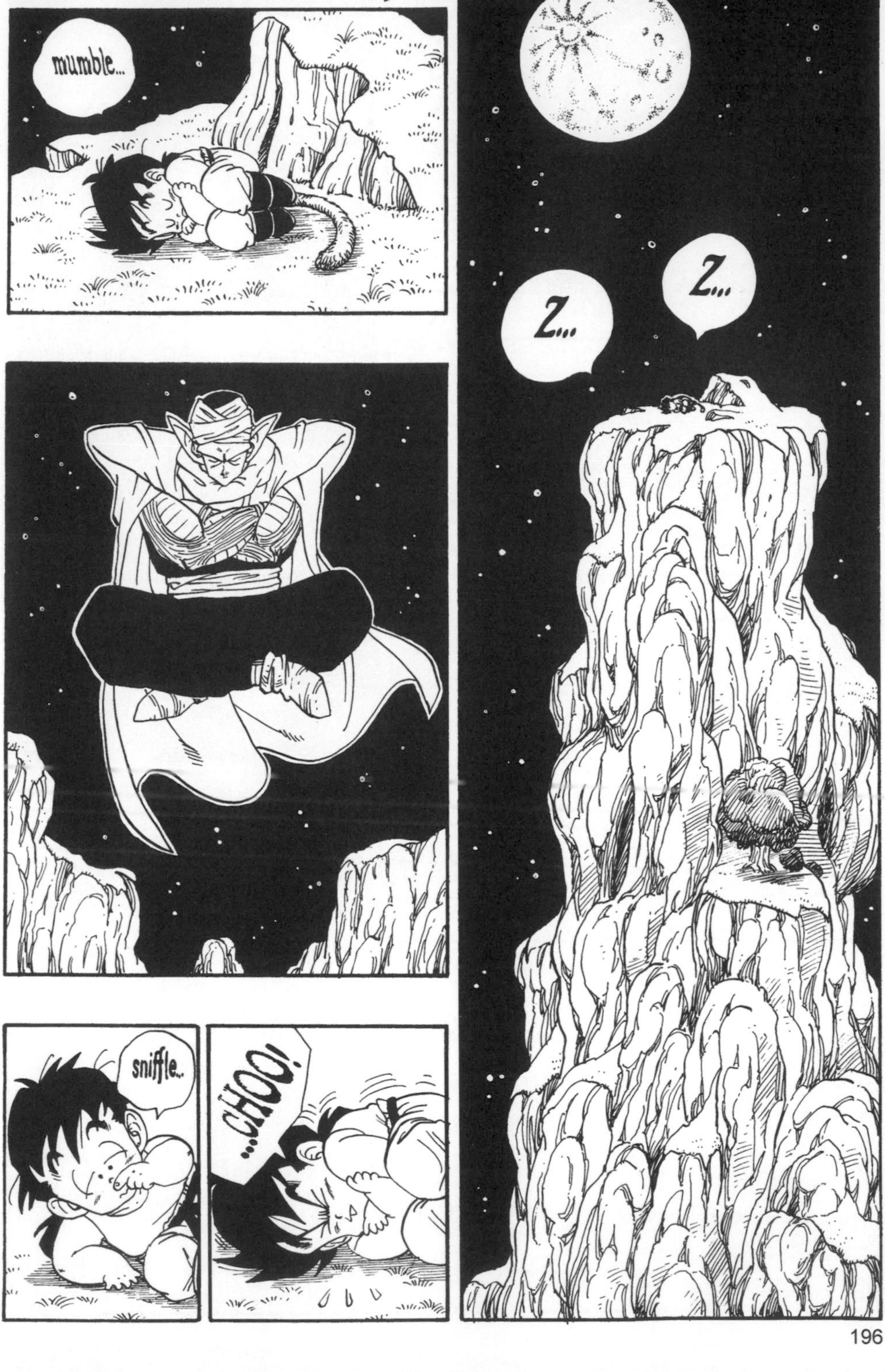

OOF

?!

tinkle

THE NEEDS OF THE BODY...

WHAT SHOULD I DO...?
I CAN'T GET DOWN FROM HERE...
...BUT IF I STAY HERE, I'LL STARVE TO DEATH...

sniff...
WHY IS THIS HAPPENING TO ME...?

?

HUH...?
WHY IS IT SO BRIGHT WHEN IT'S NIGHT...?

OH!

IT'S THE MOON!
WOW, IT'S SO ROUND! I'VE NEVER SEEN THE FULL...

M...
...

BA-BUMP
BA-BUMP
BA-BUMP
BA-BUMP
BA-BUMP
BA-BUMP

BA-BUMP
BA-BUMP
BA-BUMP
BA-BUMP

?!
WHAT IN THE WORLD...?!

RRIP
RRIP

GRAUGH!!

AA-R
K'LATTA
K'LATTA

WHAT ?!

WH-WHAT *IS* THAT...?!!

S...MP

GRRR...

WHAM!

FASH!

KA-BOOOM
Unh !!!

BOOM
BOOM

WH-WHAT'S GOING ON?!! SUCH DESTRUCTIVE POWER...!

A-AT THIS RATE, THE EARTH WILL BE DESTROYED *BEFORE* THE SAIYANS ARRIVE...!!

ONLY WHEN A MOON SHOWS ITS FULL FACE DO WE SAIYANS SHOW OUR TRUE POWERS!!

BE GONE-!!!
THAT'S IT!!
THE FULL MOON!!

VWOOSH
...G...
SHOOP...
DMP

TMP

HUFF HUFF...
HUFF...

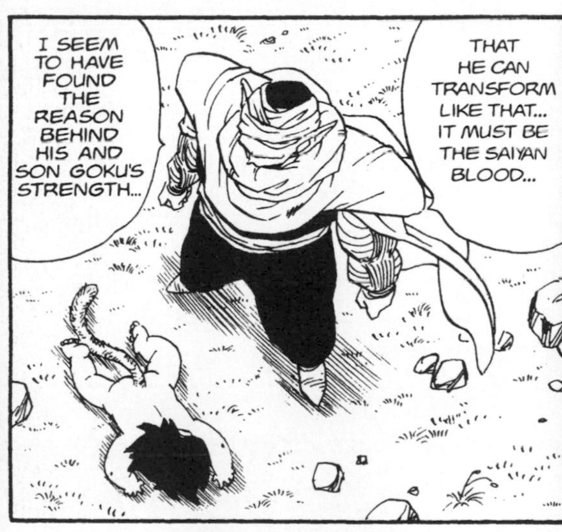
THAT HE CAN TRANSFORM LIKE THAT... IT MUST BE THE SAIYAN BLOOD...
I SEEM TO HAVE FOUND THE REASON BEHIND HIS AND SON GOKU'S STRENGTH...

IT SEEMS I WAS RIGHT IN REMOVING THE MOON'S EFFECT...
I SHUDDER TO THINK WHAT WOULD HAPPEN IF THOSE SAIYANS TRANSFORM LIKE THAT...

HE WAS SAYING SOMETHING ABOUT THE TAIL—IT SEEMS THAT BOTH A FULL MOON AND THE TAIL ARE NECESSARY FOR THE TRANSFOR-MATION...

SHOULD I REMOVE THE TAIL TOO...?
THERE'S NO NEED FOR CONCERN NOW, BUT IT SEEMS THAT THE TAIL IS THE WEAKNESS FOR SAIYANS...

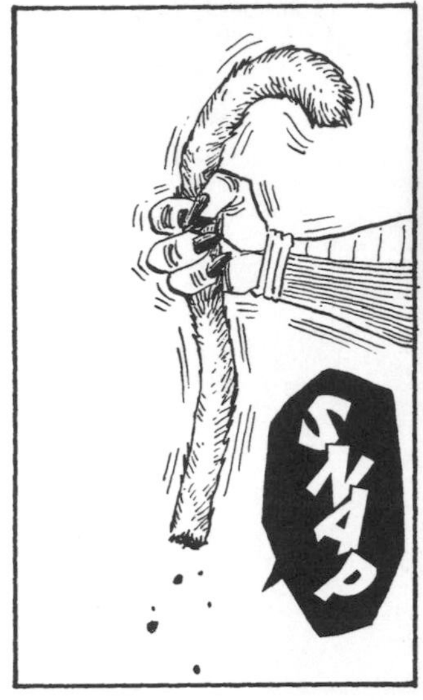
SNAP

VERY WELL...
SOME GARMENTS AND A BLADE SEEM WARRANTED...

THE SAME GUISE AS YOUR SIRE SHOULD SERVE...
ZAP

...THOUGH THE SIGIL SHOULD SEND ITS OWN MESSAGE...

SO MUCH SO THAT YOU SHALL THINK YOU WERE BETTER OFF DEAD...

PREPARE YOURSELF...

...FOR...

YOU ARE ABOUT TO BE REMADE IN MY OWN IMAGE...!

WHOOSH

Z...

Z...

DBZ:15 • Goku and Gohan's Training Begins!!

PBBBBBB

SHPPPP!!!!
NOW, CHI-CHI, DON'T GET SO UPSET...
STUFF IT, DAD!

I TOLD THEM—BE BACK BY DARK!

GOKU HASN'T BEEN TO THE TURTLE HUT IN A DOG'S AGE...
PROBABLY HAD A LOTTA CATCHIN' UP T'DO... LOST ALL TRACK O' TIME...

WELL, GOODIE FOR GOKU.
EXCEPT OUR SON HAS SCHOOL!!

BUT GOHAN'S ONLY FOUR YEARS OLD...! HE CAN MISS A DAY OF PRESCHOOL AND IT WON'T MAKE ANY—
GET WITH THE TIMES, POP!! IT'S A COMPETITIVE WORLD—AND IT'S NEVER TOO EARLY TO GET AN EDGE!!!

KAME HOUSE

CHAK CHAK
CHIK CHIK

YAWWW...

CHIK
CHAK

PI PIPI
!!

HEY!!!
I DID IT!!!

...
ZZZ..
SNXX... SNXX...

BRA-A-A-A-AT!!

IF I DON'T GET ANY SLEEP WHILE I'M FIXING THIS THING...
...THEN NOBODY'S GETTING ANY SLEEP !!!
...

HEY, YOU. TURTLE LOVER.
GET UP!
CHIK

"T-TURTLE... LOVER"...?

I SWITCHED IT OVER TO OUR NUMERIC SYSTEM, SO...
LET'S SEE... 139...!
PI PI PI
A READING OF YOUR PERSONAL POWER LEVEL!

139...!
THAT'S IMPRESSIVE... HOW DOES IT WORK?
WHAT ABOUT *MY* POWER, BULMA, WHAT ABOUT *MINE* ?!

KURIRIN IS...
WHOA-HO-*HO* !!
IT'S 206 !!
FIGH
206
SET

206 !
I COULD KICK YOU AROUND THE BLOCK!
ARE YOU *SURE* THAT THING'S FIXED...?

THE BEST THING ABOUT THIS SAIYAN SOUVENIR IS THAT IT SPOTS POWERFUL PEOPLE ALL OVER THE WORLD...AND TELLS YOU RIGHT WHERE THEY ARE!!
PI PI!!!!!

HUH?! THERE'S A 250... ABOUT 3000 KM AWAY!
WHO COULD THAT BE ?!
250 ?!

I *KNOW* !!
IT'S TEN-SHINHAN !!!

A 177... OVER THERE...
...I'M GUESSING YAMCHA... !!

AND....... A....... 329..... ?!!
P!|!
B-BUT WHO... WHAT... ?!

IT'S GOT TO BE PIC-COLO...
OH YEAH !!
TH-THEN GOHAN MUST BE THERE TOO...!

SH-SH-SHOULD WE G-GO SAVE HIM?!
MY HEART SAYS YES...
BUT MY BRAIN SAYS THAT PICCOLO TOOK GOKU'S CHILD AS PART OF A LARGER PLAN TO SAVE THE EARTH...

ANYWAY, WHAT DO YOU THINK WOULD HAPPEN IF WE *DID* TRY TO SAVE HIM?
...
HE'S 329... HE'D *SLAUGHTER* US...

BUT NOW, THANKS TO THIS, WE'LL BE ABLE TO FIND YAMCHA AND EVERYBODY ELSE!
IF WE SPLIT UP, THE OTHER SIX DRAGON BALLS'LL BE A CINCH TO FIND! WE'LL BE ABLE TO BRING GOKU BACK TO LIFE IN NO TIME!!

YO !!!
I SAY, "YO" !!!
CAPSULE

IS THAT A VOICE OR A FALLING LOG...?
KRII
'SME...
HEY! YOU'RE THE ONE WHO WAS AT KARIN'S PLACE... UM...ITCHY-ROBE!!
YAJIROBE, IDIOT !!
YOU DID THAT ON PURPOSE !!

THIS IS A STUPID PLACE FOR A HOUSE !
KARIN DIDN' TELL ME IT WAS GONNA TAKE SO LONG T'FIND YA!
KARIN...?!

HE KNOWS WUZZUP.
HE SAYS YOU AN' THE YAMCHA GUY... AND TEN-SOMETHIN'...AND CHAOZU...GET OVER THERE NOW!

EVERY-BODY...AT KARIN'S...?
WHY ?!
WHO IS IT?

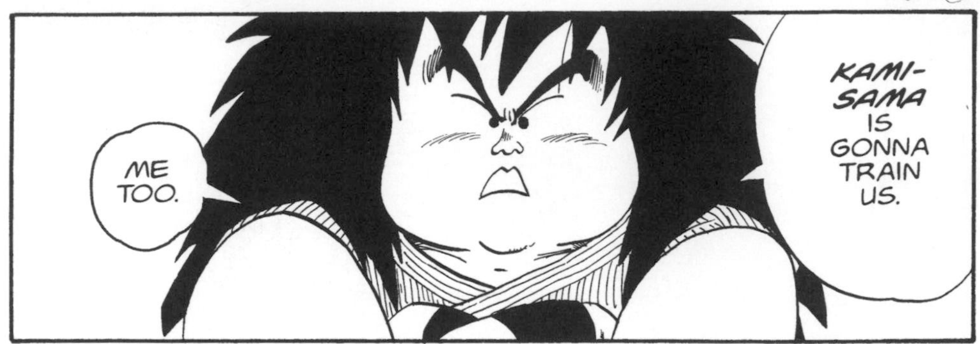
KAMI-SAMA IS GONNA TRAIN US.
ME TOO.

H-HE-HE-WHAT ?!
YEAH. I SAID I DIDN'T WANT TO FIGHT THOSE WHADDYA-CALLEM ALIENS, BUT KARIN...

WE'LL BE THERE !!
ALL OF US!! RIGHT AWAY !!

LATER.
I DONE WHAT I WAS S'POSE TA.

OH YEAH! ALMOST F'RGOT !
HE SAID DON'T BRING GOKU BACK TO LIFE 'TIL THE BAD GUYS GET HERE.
CAPSULE

WHAT ?!
B-BUT WHY... ?!

HE'S TRAININ' IN HELL.
ASK THE OLD WITCH.

BYOO...

HUH...
?
HE'S COMING BACK...
?

NO...
GYOOO...
IT'S NOT HIM...

T-TRAINING... IN H-HELL...
?!
OH MY, OH MY...

HOWDY-DOO
!!!
MASTER, MASTER, IT'S ME!!!

GAA
!!!!
NOT GYŪ-MAŌ... AND CHI-CHI
!!!

HOW ARE YOU, MASTER?! IT'S BEEN SO LONG !!
HUH...? OH... YEAH. F-FINE...
OHHHHH... MAMA... !!

SO WHERE'S MY SON, HMM ?
WHERE'D GOKU TAKE HIM NOW ?

WELL...UM...
A-ACTUALLY... HEH HEH...

...TAKEN... BY PICCOLO ?!!!

WHAT WAS **GOKU** DOING WHEN THIS HAPPENED?!

...DYING... MOSTLY...

......

DONK!
CHI-CHI !!!

SIX MONTHS PASS (AND ***FAST***, HUH?)...

YAMCHA AND TENSHINHAN WERE EASILY FOUND, AND THEY HAVE TOILED EVERY DAY UNDER THE STRICT TRAINING OF KAMI-SAMA...

AS FOR SON GOKU... HE'S STILL RUNNING... AND RUNNING...AND RUNNING...TOWARD KAIŌ-SAMA, THE "LORD OF WORLDS"...
ZEEH
ZEEH

AND HOW ABOUT SON GOHAN?!

GOLP GOLP...
WELL, HE SEEMS TO BE SURVIVING!

HRR?
?!

OH, YOU AGAIN...
YOU DON'T GIVE UP EASY, DO YA?

RAAAR !!!
BOING

GRAUGH!!
JOONG
JOONG

NYAAA-NYAAA !

CHMMM

D NK

THM

VSHH
OH, BOY!! TIME FOR ANOTHER SLICE!!!

GUH...

HEY, DON'T LIZARDS' TAILS GROW *BACK* ?!

BWOO

HSH...
POP POPPLE

HMPH... HE SEEMS TO BE GETTING THIS DOWN...
WELL, THEN...IT'S TIME TO BEGIN TESTING HIM FOR REAL...

DBZ:16 • Masters and Students

TYAH!!!!

WH-
WHERE
DID...
?!

VZZZ
SHP

WAAH!!!
GNG
LOOK
AROUND
YOU!

HE...
HE
DISAPPEARED...
!!!

YOU WENT TOO FAST...I COULDN'T SEE YOU...!
DON'T TRY TO SEE.
JUST... *FEEL*.

I DON'T KNOW WHAT YOU MEAN...
MUTTER MUTTER
IT'S NOT FAIR THAT WAY...
IF I CAN'T SEE YOU...
fap fap

PI

BACH
YOW!!

IF YOU HAVE TIME TO COMPLAIN, THEN YOU HAVE TIME TO *ACT*!!

REMEMBER!
YOU HAVE ONLY SIX MORE MONTHS.

YOU WILL SLEEP, YOU WILL EAT... AND YOU WILL FIGHT WITH ME!
PREPARE YOURSELF.
HUH ?!

WOBBLE OBBLE
B-B-BUT...
...BUT I'LL DIE...

OR BECOME *STRONG*.
STRONGER THAN *ME*...
...AND THE SAIYANS WHO COME TO DESTROY US.

...

DO YOU CALL THAT A DEFENSE ?! CONCENTRATE !
I'M DYING TO KILL YOU, YOU KNOW!
BA!
BA!
BA!
BA!
ACK !
ACK !

huff huff
huff huff

MEANWHILE, GOKU RUNS... AND RUNS... AND RUNS...ALONG THE SERPENT ROAD... UNTIL FINALLY...

YEESH... HOW...
H-HOW MUCH LONGER... I-IS THIS R-ROAD GONNA GO ON...?
AT THIS RATE...THE YEAR'LL BE GONE...BEFORE I EVEN SEE THIS LORD OF...

huff huff
ZEEH ZEEH

?!

WAAAA!!!!
I DID IT!!! I'M HERE!!!
IT'S THE TAIL!!!

...IS NO-
WHERE...
EXCEPT
HERE...

...

SOME
ROUND
THING...

EH
?!

IT
CAN'T
BE...!
TH-
THERE'S
GOTTA
BE...!

WAHOO
!!!!
BOOM

THAT'S
IT
!!!!
HE
MUST
BE UP
THERE
!!!

I KNEW IT!!

A HOUSE !!!

L-LIKE... I'M BEING PRESSED DOWN... B-BY SOME FORCE... !!
LIKE MY WHOLE B-BODY... IS LEAD... !!

OH!

THAT MUST BE... KAIŌ-SAMA?
HE'S GOT A...A STRANGE FORM, BUT...

G-GREETINGS! I AM SON GOKU!
I SEEK TRAINING FROM YOU!

ZOOP

!!

OOKA OOKA
OOKA OOKA

OOKA OOKA
OOKA OOKA
THIS M-MUST BE THE TRAINING !!
I'D BETTER FOLLOW !!

OOKA OOKA... OOKA OOKA...
IT'S SO...SO HARD... !
L-LORD OF WORLDS... WHAT'S WITH THIS GROUND...?
OOKA OOKA
OOKA OOKA

OOKA... OOKA... !
OOKA... OOKA !!

AND HERE I THOUGHT...
...*HE* WAS THE MONKEY.

HUH ?
...

WH-
WHO...
?
WH-
WH-
WHAT...?
HEH
HEH
HEH
HEH...

NNNNG...
THESE
BITES...
ALWAYS
SO
MANY...
...FLIES
AROUND
ME...
HEH
HEH...

SCRITCHA SCRITCHA

WHAT
?!
TH-
THEN
WHO'S...
?!
OOKA
...OOKA
...
THAT?
THAT'S
BUBBLES.

I AM
THE
LORD
OF
WORLDS
!

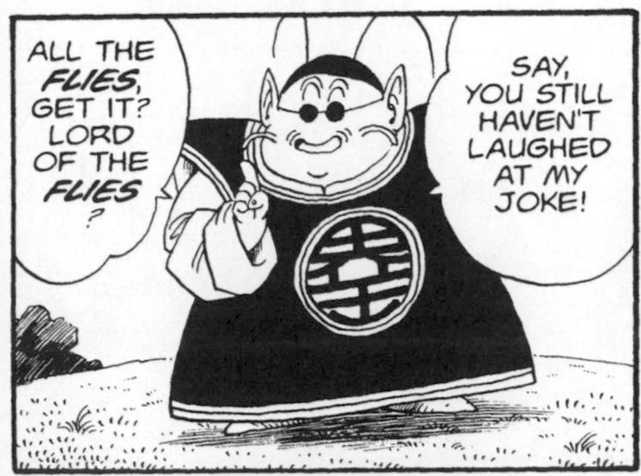
SAY,
YOU STILL
HAVEN'T
LAUGHED
AT MY
JOKE!
ALL THE
FLIES,
GET IT?
LORD
OF THE
FLIES
?

HEH HEH...
I THOUGHT
THAT WAS
WEIRD...
YOU
THOUGHT
IT WAS
WEIRD?!

UM... WHAT... ?
...
OH...I GET IT... TOO NERVOUS TO LAUGH, EH?

OF COURSE... THAT'S UNDER-STANDABLE...
LET'S TRY ANOTHER ONE! LET'S SEE...

DO YOU HAVE PIG'S FEET ?
YES, I DO.
WEAR SHOES AND MAYBE NOBODY'LL NOTICE !

HEE *HEE*... *SNORT*
OH, THAT WAS A GOOD ONE!
A...A GOOD WHAT... ?

.....

YOU CAME FOR A *REASON*, I SUPPOSE?
YEAH !
I WANT TO BE TRAINED BY YOU!

FORGET IT!
IF YOU'RE TOO STUPID TO LAUGH AT A GREAT JOKE LIKE THAT...
...THERE'S NOTHING I CAN TEACH YOU!!

BWAA HA HAA !!
THAT'S A GOOD ONE!! WHAT A JOKE !!
THE LORD O' JOKES, THAT'S YOU!!

...HEH...
...I AM, AREN'T I...?
GUESS YOU'RE JUST A LITTLE SLOW...
SO YOU WILL?

TRAIN YOU, EH...? HEH HEH HEH...
OKAY, I'LL DO IT...
...IF YOU CAN PASS THE TEST!

IF YOU CAN MAKE ME, THE WIT OF WORLDS...
...LAUGH AT A JOKE OF YOURS!!

HUH?!
B-BUT I'M NO COMEDIAN...!!

IT'S YOUR ONLY HOPE...
...AND I ONLY LAUGH AT THE MOST SOPHIS-TICATED HUMOR!
I...I DON'T KNOW...

I THOUGHT SO...
HAVE A NICE RUN HOME!

I-I-I DON'T EVEN KNOW WHAT COMEDIANS READ!!
COMIC BOOKS?!!!

DOOOOM

WH-WHAT COMEDIANS READ...
..."COMIC BOOKS"?

PFT
SNORT

TEEEE HEE HEE...
HOO HOO HOO !!!

I DID IT !!!!
I MADE YOU LAUGH !!!!

C-CURSE IT ALL... HEE HEE
"NOT A COMEDIAN," HE SAYS...!
I GOTTA REMEMBER THAT ONE.

IT IS SO! I SHALL TRAIN YOU!
YOU SHALL BE A MASTER OF HUMOR!
HUMOR...? WHO WANTS HUMOR?! I WANT MARTIAL ARTS LESSONS!

OH, MARTIAL ARTS.
WHY DIDN'T YOU SAY SO?

ALL RIGHT, TRY TO ATTACK ME.
LET'S SEE HOW GOOD YOU ARE.
UM... I'D LOVE TO, BUT...
I FEEL SO HEAVY HERE... I CAN HARDLY MOVE!

WHERE ARE YOU FROM, EARTH?
UH-HUH...

NO WONDER.
THIS IS A SMALL PLANET, BUT IT HAS POWERFUL GRAVITY.
ABOUT TEN TIMES THAT OF YOUR WORLD—SO YOU WEIGH TEN TIMES AS MUCH!

TRY TO JUMP UP.
AS HIGH AS YOU CAN!
O-OKAY...

HYAA!!
BMM

UNGH! IT'S...NO GOOD!!
I CAN HARDLY... GET UP!
DMM

HMM... JUMPING THAT FAR... IN TEN TIMES HIS USUAL GRAVITY...!
THIS IS GOING TO BE INTERESTING...!!

DBZ:17 • The Hardest Time of His Death

AT LAST, GOKU'S FOUND THE LORD OF THE WORLDS AND BEGGED HIM FOR COMBAT TRAINING! TOO BAD IT'LL HAVE TO HAPPEN ON THIS TINY PLANET WITH GRAVITY TEN TIMES THAT OF EARTH!

OKAY, I'LL GIVE YOU THE LESSONS...
...BUT HOW MUCH TIME DO YOU HAVE?
I DON'T KNOW HOW MANY DAYS I SPENT RUNNING ON THE SERPENT ROAD... BUT I DON'T THINK THERE ARE MANY LEFT...
THESE SAIYAN GUYS ARE COMING TO EARTH...TO DESTROY IT!
JUST TEACH ME AS MUCH AS YOU CAN, IN THE TIME I'VE GOT.

SAIYANS, HUH?
SOUNDS LIKE YOU'VE GOT A REAL PROBLEM ON YOUR HANDS...
LET'S SEE...
pwik
MAYBE I CAN LEARN WHEN THEY'RE DUE ON EARTH...

HMM... WE'VE GOT SOME FLYING SAIYANS, ALL RIGHT...
ON A PACE TO REACH EARTH IN... OH, SAY... 158 DAYS...
WOW!
THAT'S AMAZING!! HOW—

WAIT...
ONLY 158 DAYS?

OH, DON'T WORRY.
IT'LL BE MORE THAN ENOUGH.

BUT... BUT...
158 DAYS WITH ME...
...IS LIKE A FEW THOUSAND YEARS OF TRAINING ON EARTH.

FOR ***REAL*** ?!

OF COURSE, THAT STILL DOESN'T MEAN YOU'RE GOING TO ***WIN*** AGAINST THEM.
THOSE TWO SAIYANS ARE VERY, ***VERY*** STRONG.

MATTER OF FACT, THEY'RE STRONGER THAN ME!
WAK !!
STR- STRONGER THAN... ?!

YOU GOT IT.
SO TO BEAT THEM, YOU'LL HAVE TO OUTDO ME... AT THE VERY LEAST!

...

SHALL WE GET STARTED ?
HEY, BUBBLES !

OO-OO-OO
OO-OO-OO

UNTIL YOU CAN OVER-COME THIS GRAVITY...
...THERE'S NO POINT IN ANYTHING ELSE!
YOUR FIRST LESSON IS SIMPLY TO CATCH BUBBLES!
OKAY...

OOP OOP
UNGH !!
DM
DM
STOP !!

OOK
EEK
RRGH!! 'SIMPOSSIBLE !
I-I CAN'T BE THIS HEAVY... !

OKAY... NGH... YOU!
JUST... YOU... WAIT !

RRRG !

DOOOM
HUFF HUFF

NKH!! NKH!!
I'LL CATCH YOU... !!

GEH HEH HEH... !!
NOW I'LL GET YOU!!

HYAARH !!
DM DM DM DM

OH-HO !
EXTRA WEIGHTS ON HIM, EH...?

VWMM
UH ?!

GOTCHA !!

GOMP
NUH... NO...IT CAN'T BE...
OOPA OOPA
EEKA EEKA

HE'S TOO FAST...
I...I DUNNO IF I'LL EVER B-BE ABLE TO...
...OKAY, FINE. GO HOME.

W-WAIT... CAN I GET SOME-THING TO EAT...?
I HAVEN'T EATEN IN SIX MONTHS, AND I'M STARVING.

WELL... I GUESS...
...ALTHOUGH YOU'RE THE FIRST HUNGRY DEAD MAN I EVER HEARD OF...

GLUMP
SHRP...
!!
HEY!! HEY!!
YOU EVER HEAR THE PHRASE "SLOW DOWN"?!

HWOO!! I'M STUFFED !!
THE TASTE AIN'T MUCH, BUT AT LEAST THERE'S A LOT!
DIDN'T GET A LOT OF ETIQUETTE TRAINING, DID YOU...?

SAY...DON'T YOU GET BORED ON THIS TINY PLANET...?
AH, FOOLISH YOUTH...

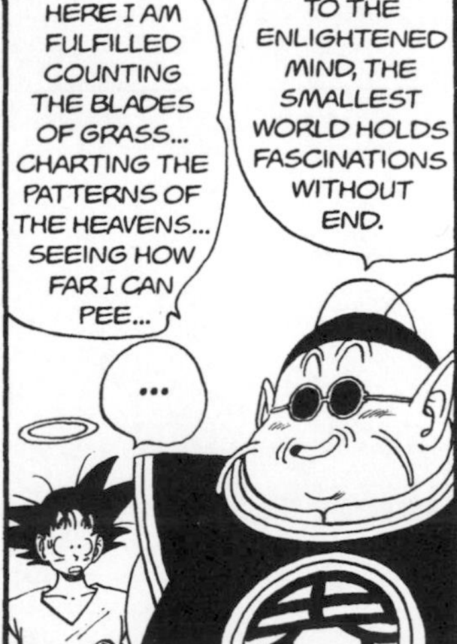
TO THE ENLIGHTENED MIND, THE SMALLEST WORLD HOLDS FASCINATIONS WITHOUT END.
HERE I AM FULFILLED COUNTING THE BLADES OF GRASS... CHARTING THE PATTERNS OF THE HEAVENS... SEEING HOW FAR I CAN PEE...
...

MY LATEST OCCUPATION...
...IS DRIVING.

"DRIVING"... RIGHT...

NOW GET OUT THERE AND CATCH THE MONKEY.
OTHERWISE, OUR TRAINING STOPS RIGHT HERE!
OHHH-KAY... I'LL DO MY BEST...!

OH YES, AND PUT THOSE HEAVY CLOTHES AND SHOES BACK ON.
IT'LL BE BETTER EXERCISE THAT WAY.
HUH ?!

B-BUT WITH THOSE ON ME...
...I CAN HARDLY EVEN MOVE... !!

LET ME TELL YOU SOME-THING...
THE HOMEWORLD OF THE SAIYANS HAS GRAVITY AT LEAST AS GREAT AS THIS...

...

DO YOU BEGIN TO SEE WHERE THEY GET THEIR STRENGTH FROM?
AND THAT ISN'T EVEN TO MENTION THEIR INBORN FIGHTING INSTINCTS...
YOU CAN'T EVEN IMAGINE HOW DEADLY THEY ARE...

SURE I CAN!
I MEAN, I'M SAIYAN, TOO!

EH ?!

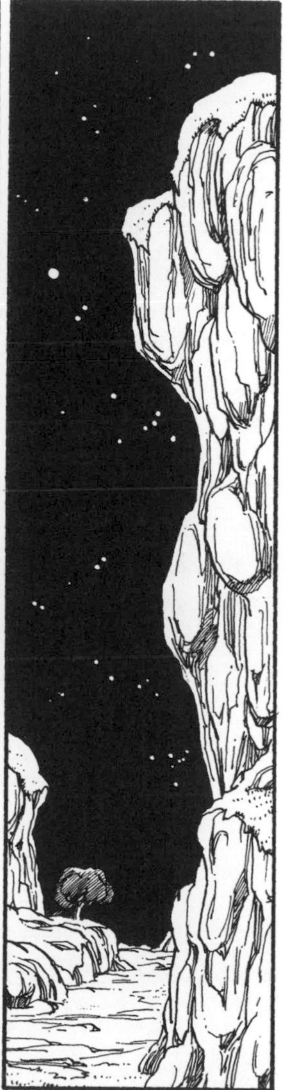

OHH...
OWWW...

FEH...
AT LEAST THE LAST SIX MONTHS HAVE TAUGHT YOU NOT TO BE A CRYBABY...
HEH... HEH HEH...

HEY...YOU FOUGHT MY DADDY BEFORE, DIDN'T YOU?

AND I WILL AGAIN...
IF WE CAN BEAT THE SAIYANS, IT WILL BE HIS TURN NEXT...

BUT DADDY USED TO SAY...
...YOU'RE NOT AS BAD OF A BAD GUY AS YOU USED TO BE, BEFORE YOU DIED AND CAME BACK.

HMPH...

I THINK HE'S RIGHT...
...BUT MOMMY AND GRANDPA WERE SURE SCARED OF YOU...

...

SHUT UP AND GO TO SLEEP!
I WILL NOT MAKE TOMORROW... AS EASY AS TODAY!
Y-YESSIR!

ZZ
ZZ

...LITTLE BRAT...!

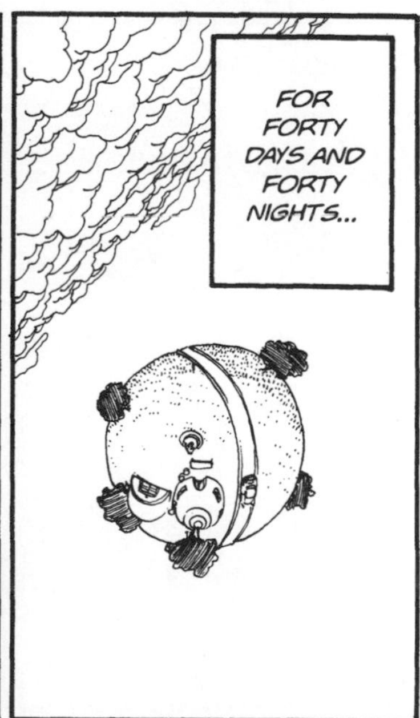
FOR FORTY DAYS AND FORTY NIGHTS...

NRRR!

BWA

GMP

OH !!

I DID IT !!!
I FINALLY CAUGHT 'IM !!!!
MAGNIFICENT!

HE QUICKLY OVERCAME THIS PLANET'S GRAVITY...
HE REALLY *IS* AS GREAT AS I'D HOPED...

AND STILL 118 DAYS REMAINING! HE MAY BE THE ONE WHO CAN MASTER THE KAIŌ-KEN... !!!

THE KAIŌ-KEN THAT I HAVE YEARNED OF... BUT COULD NEVER MASTER MYSELF...!!!! OH, FOR THAT FINAL ATTACK...!!!!

SO, YOU THINK YOU'RE READY?! WELL, MY TRAINING IS TOUGHER THAN YOU CAN IMAGINE!!!
DO YOU REALLY THINK YOU CAN **TAKE** IT?!!
I'M READY !!!

YOU HAVE TO BE THE **BEST**!!! THE GREATEST FIGHTER IN THE UNIVERSE!!!
PHYSICALLY!!! MENTALLY!!! IN EVERY WAY!!!

I'M **READY** !!!

LET'S HAVE SOME TEA FIRST...
WOOOM

YOU HAVE ALL SURPASSED ME NOW.
THERE IS NOTHING MORE I OR MR. POPO CAN TEACH YOU.
RETURN TO THE LOWER WORLD AND REFINE YOUR SKILLS UNTIL THE FINAL CONFRONTATION.

I LEAVE THE FUTURE TO YOU.

YES, SIR!
CAN I TAKE THIS WEIGHTED SHIRT OFF NOW?

—YES!!! YOU'RE GAINING CONTROL OF YOUR ENERGY!!!

IT'S NOT ENOUGH!!!
WAM

IT'S NO USE...
EVEN I CAN'T READ THE FUTURE THIS TIME...

AND SO THE BATTLE HOUR DRAWS NEAR...!

DBZ:18 • Closer...Closer...

THEN LET'S BEGIN.
CATCH A GIANT BRICK...AT SUPER SPEED!
OKAY !

TYAH!!
HUUN

CHOOOM

HWSH

HAI-
YAAH
!!!!
SUPER-
SUPER
SPEED
!!!

KIIIIII------N

YA

SHABOOOM

HE...
...HE DID IT...

SPLENDID, SON GOKU!
I NEVER DARED HOPE YOU'D MASTER THE "GENKI-DAMA" SPIRIT BALL SO QUICKLY!
I WORKED HARD.

REMEMBER THAT THE "SPIRIT BALL" IS A MARTIAL-ARTS DISCIPLINE THAT ALLOWS YOU TO BORROW ENERGY FROM GRASS AND TREES, FROM PEOPLE AND ANIMALS, FROM INANIMATE OBJECTS AND THE ATMOSPHERE... AND THEN TO CONCENTRATE THEM AND RELEASE THEM.
IF YOU CAN DRAW SO MUCH DESTRUCTIVE POWER FROM A BALL MADE ON THIS SMALL PLANET...

...IMAGINE WHAT YOU CAN DO WITH A SPIRIT BALL FORMED ON EARTH! IF YOU CAN ALSO LEARN TO TAP INTO THE ASTOUNDING POWERS OF THE SUN...
WELL. JUST BE CAREFUL. OR YOU MAY END UP DESTROYING THE VERY PLANET YOU'RE TRYING TO PROTECT!

DON'T USE IT IF YOU CAN AVOID IT! I GIVE YOU PERMISSION TO USE IT JUST *ONCE*, WHEN THERE IS NO ALTERNATIVE.
UNDER-STAND...?

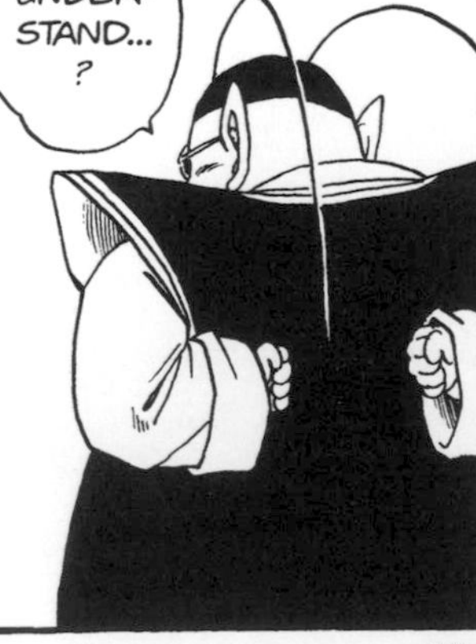

NO PROBLEM!
I'LL JUST MAKE DO WITH THE KAIŌ-KEN!

THE DAY OF THE BATTLE HAS FINALLY COME.
THE SAIYANS WILL REACH EARTH TOMORROW, AND...

OH!!

WAH !!!!
NO, NO, NO !!!!!

WHAT IS IT?!
WHAT'S **WRONG** ?!
I FORGOT TO FACTOR IN THE TIME IT'D TAKE YOU TO GO **BACK** ON THE SERPENT ROAD...

Y-Y-YOU MEAN YOU CAN'T JUST **FLY** ME TO EARTH?!
I HAVE TO GO BY THE ROAD AGAIN?! B-BUT IT TOOK ME SIX MONTHS TO GET HERE!!!

AT YOUR CURRENT SPEED YOU'LL MAKE IT IN TWO DAYS!! I'LL TELL THE EARTH-LORD TO PICK YOU UP!
BUT THAT'S STILL A DAY **LATE**!!! EARTH WILL BE **DESTROYED** !!!

OKAY, SO I MADE A **MISTAKE** !!
NOW TELL YOUR FRIENDS ON EARTH TO BRING YOU BACK TO LIFE WITH THOSE DRAGON BALLS!!!

T-TELL THEM? HOW?
PUT ONE HAND ON MY BACK AND REACH FOR THEM WITH YOUR MIND!!

F-FOR REAL?!
LIKE THIS?
HURRY UP!

TURTLE MAN... KAME-SEN'NIN! IT'S GOKU! CAN YOU HEAR ME...?

HUH?! G-GOKU?!
WHERE ARE YOU?!

I'M IN HELL!! I MEAN, THE UNDER-WORLD!

UNDER... WORLD...?
I'M TALKING TO YOU THROUGH MY MIND!

HAVE YOU FOUND ALL THE DRAGON BALLS?
YEAH...A LONG TIME AGO! EVERY-BODY HELPED, ONCE THEY HEARD IT WAS FOR YOU...

COOL! COULD YOU SUMMON SHENLONG RIGHT AWAY AND BRING ME BACK TO LIFE...?

THE SAIYANS ARE COMING TO EARTH TOMORROW.
WHAT ?!

TOMORROW ALREADY...?! THAT'S MORE THAN A MONTH SOONER THAN WE THOUGHT...!!
SO HURRY! I'LL BE A LITTLE LATE, BUT I'LL DO EVERYTHING I CAN!

OKAY! OKAY! OKAY!
BUT GOKU... HOW ARE YOU?! WE HEARD YOU WERE TRAINING IN THE UNDERWORLD...
YEAH! IT WAS GREAT !!

SO WHAT'S WITH THE OLD TURTLE-RIDER? HE'S MUMBLING TO HIMSELF IN THE JOHN...
WHAT A TIME TO GO SENILE...

HURRY !!!
GET THE DRAGON BALLS!!!
BAMM

THAT WAS AMAZING!! HE ACTUALLY HEARD ME!!
HEH HEH... OF COURSE.
NOW...WHILE WE WAIT FOR YOU TO COME BACK TO LIFE, LET'S DO SOME-THING ABOUT THOSE RIPPED-UP CLOTHES OF YOURS...

PING
VOILA.

WOW !!
AN' THEY'RE REALLY LIGHT !!

NOT JUST LIGHT...
...BUT MADE OF A POWERFUL FABRIC THAT WILL REPEL SMALL ATTACKS.
HEY, THANKS !

AN' THE TURTLE SYMBOL'S THE SAME!
I WAS AFRAID YOU'D STICK ME WITH LAME CLOTHES LIKE YOURS!
WELL, PARDONEZ-MOI...!

I CAN'T WAIT TILL I COME BACK TO LIFE!
THE SYMBOL ON THE BACK'S AN ESPECIALLY NICE TOUCH, I THINK...

ONE WISH...
...WILL BE GRANTED YOU.

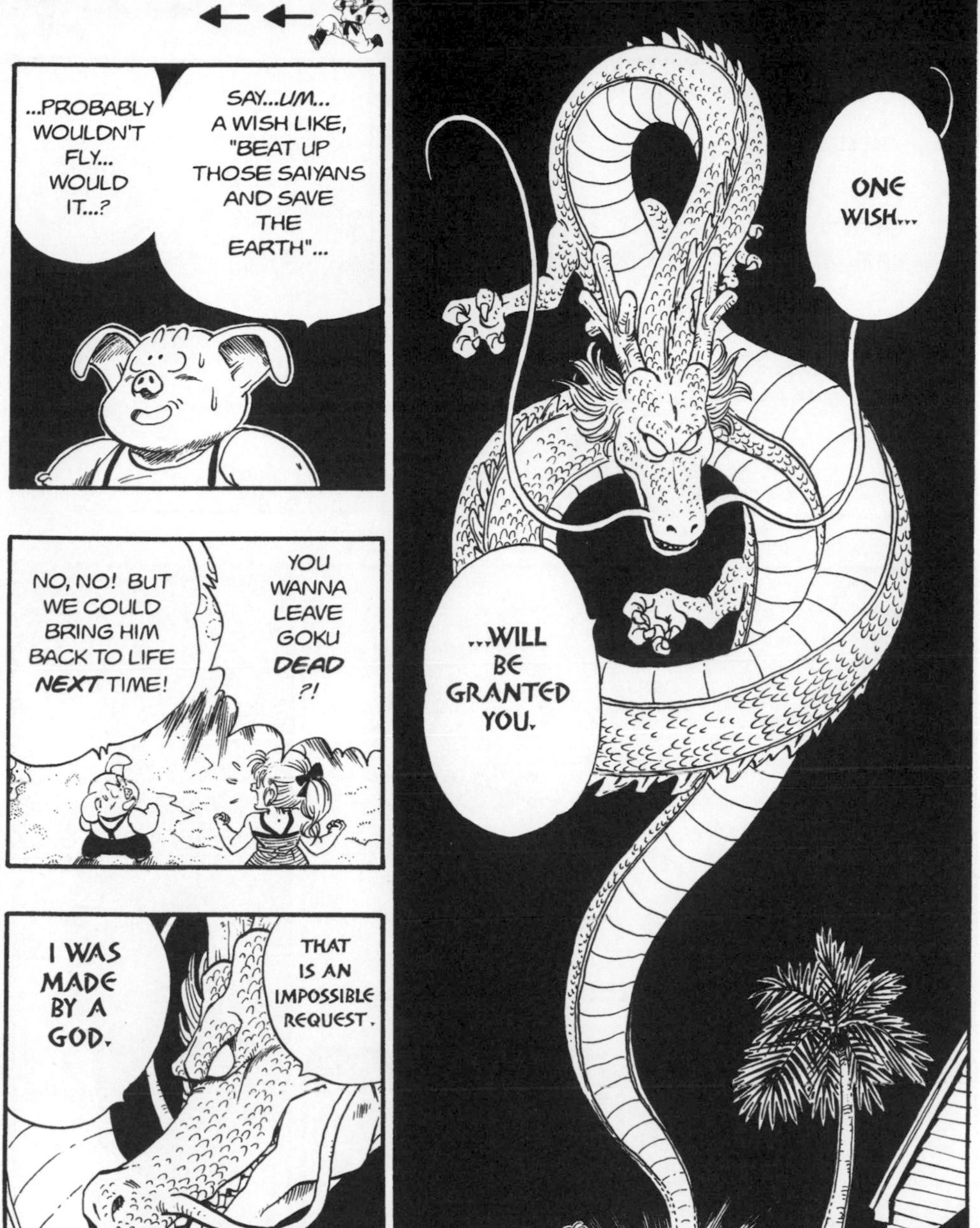

SAY...UM... A WISH LIKE, "BEAT UP THOSE SAIYANS AND SAVE THE EARTH"...
...PROBABLY WOULDN'T FLY... WOULD IT...?

YOU WANNA LEAVE GOKU DEAD?!
NO, NO! BUT WE COULD BRING HIM BACK TO LIFE NEXT TIME!

THAT IS AN IMPOSSIBLE REQUEST.
I WAS MADE BY A GOD.
I CANNOT GRANT A WISH THAT SURPASSES THE POWER OF GOD.

THEN PLEASE BRING SON GOKU BACK TO LIFE.

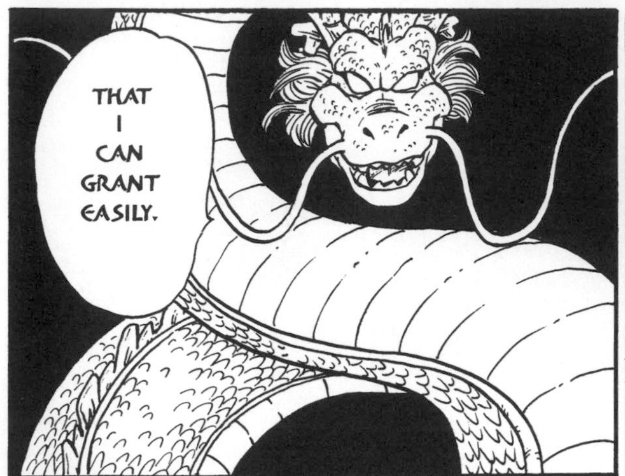

THAT I CAN GRANT EASILY.

I-IT WAS DAY...
...BUT IT GOT DARK ALL OF A SUDDEN!
!!

SO... SON GOKU RETURNS TO LIFE AT LAST...

...WHICH MUST MEAN THE SAIYANS COME SOONER THAN WE THOUGHT...

FT
HEY !!

GOOD!! THE HALO IS GONE!! YOU'RE ALIVE AGAIN!!
NOW GET GOING !!!
O-KAY !!!

REMEMBER, THE ENEMY IS MORE POWERFUL AND EVIL THAN YOU CAN IMAGINE!! YOU MUST ALWAYS BE ON YOUR GUARD!!
DON'T START THINKING THAT YOU CAN JUST COME BACK TO LIFE AGAIN!!
I KNOW, I KNOW! YOU CAN ONLY COME BACK TO LIFE ONCE! I'LL DO MY BEST!

AN' THANKS FOR EVERY-THING.
IF I DIE AGAIN, I'LL COME VISIT YOU!

G'BYE-EEE !!!

HIS POWER KNOWS NO BOUNDS... AND YET HIS SOUL IS CLEARER THAN CRYSTAL...I NEVER THOUGHT SUCH A BEING COULD EXIST IN THE CORPOREAL WORLD.
TOO BAD HIS SENSE OF HUMOR WASN'T ON THE SAME LEVEL... WELL, NEXT TIME...

WOO-HOO!! I FEEL SO LIGHT !!
POINNNG
I'M LIKE A LIVING COTTON BAAAALL !!!

WELL, NO TIME TO PLAY AROUND !!!
I'VE GOT TO GO !!!

THE NEXT DAY, AT 11:43 AM, IT HAPPENED AT LAST...

HYUUUU~~~

DOOM

DBZ:19 • The Day of the Saiyans

IT LOOKS LIKE SOMETHING FELL FROM THE SKY...
WHAT IN THE WORLD...?
MURMUR MURMUR

WERE THOSE... BOMBS?
WH-WHAT HAPPENED?

Y-YOU'RE RIGHT...!
THAT ROUND THING...! BUT WHAT...?
HERE'S ANOTHER ONE!

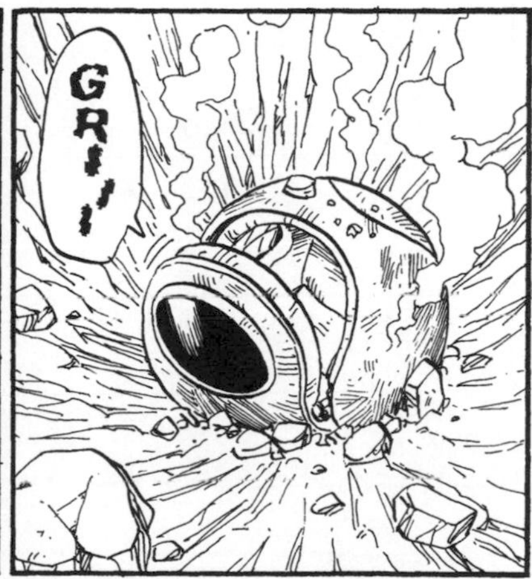

GR

IT'S A MAN !!
AND HE'S COMING OUT !!

WHEW.

!!
!!

SO... THEY'VE COME AT LAST...!
MAN... WHAT INCREDIBLE CHI!

!!

!!

...!

T-
TENSHINHAN...
!!
CURSE
THEM...
THEY CAME
SOONER
THAN WE
THOUGHT!

WHO
ARE
THEY?
YADA... YADA
WHAT
ARE
THEY?!

"EARTH,"
WAS
IT...?
PROMISING...

WE SHOULD
GREET THE
LITTLE
INSECTS...

KUNG
ZWOO

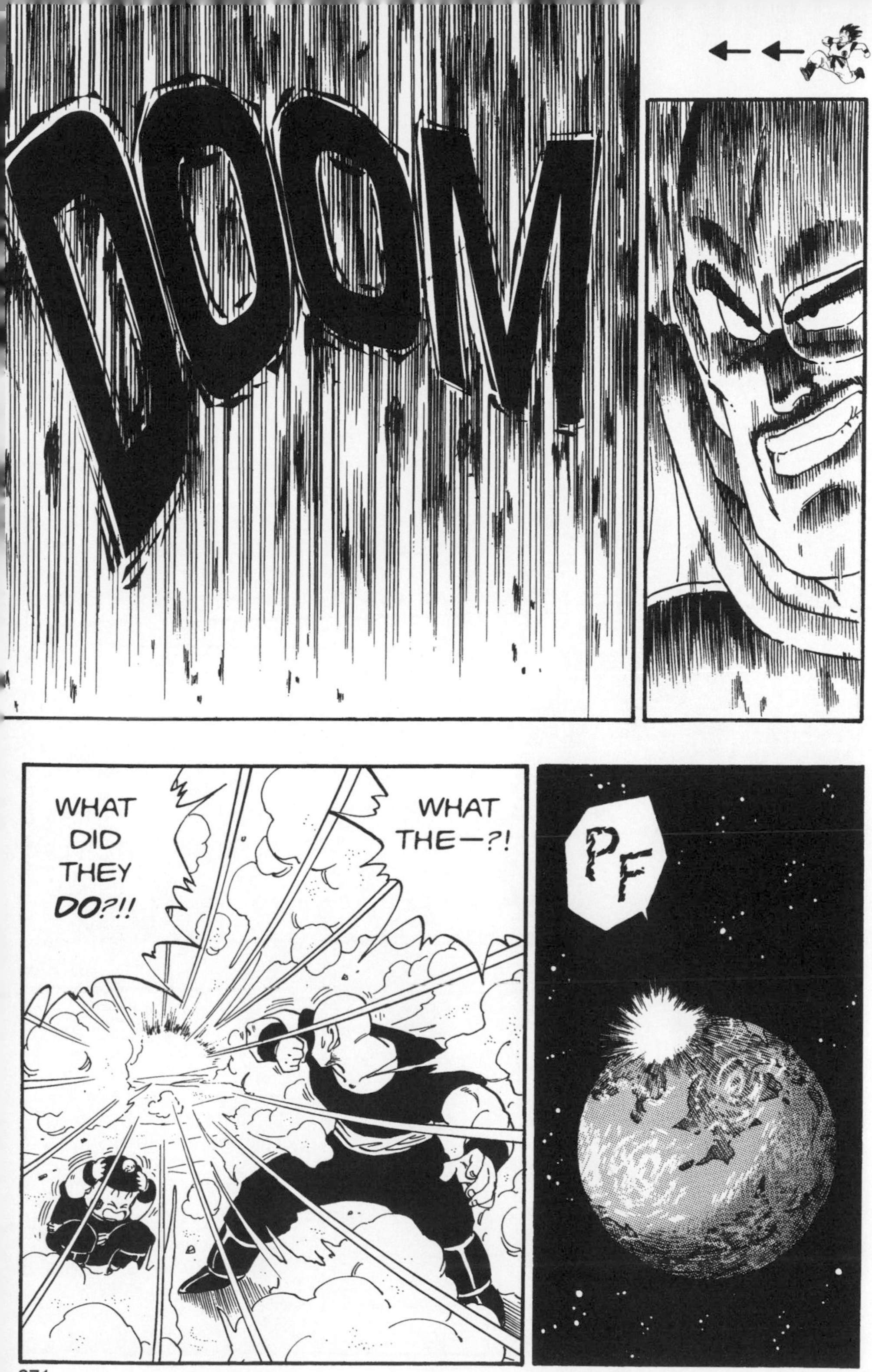

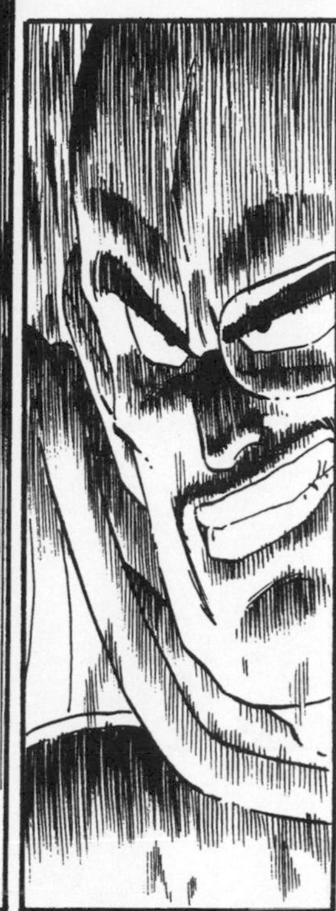

DOOM!

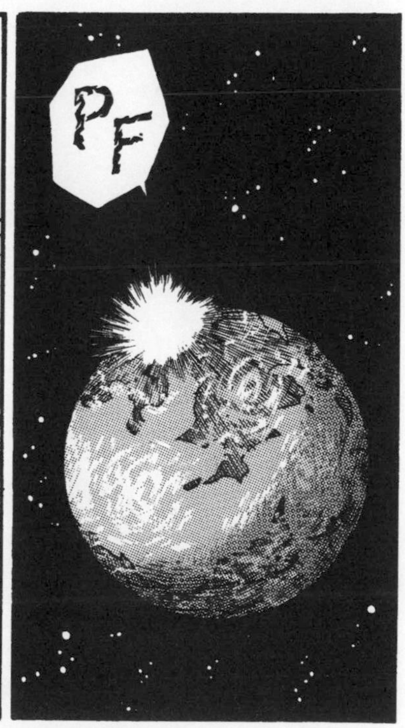
PF

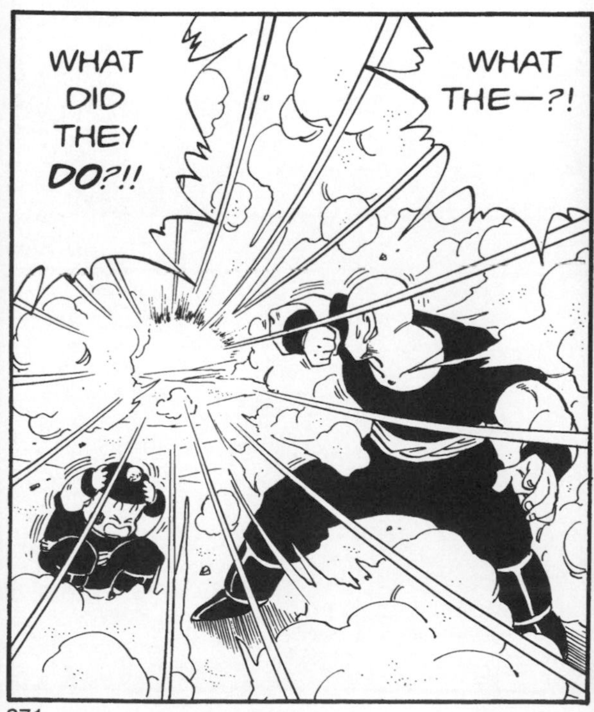
WHAT THE—?!
WHAT DID THEY DO?!!

WA HA HA-HA HA!!! A LITTLE ***TOO*** WARM A GREETING, EH, VEGETA?!

END IT THERE, NAPPA...

YOU'LL DESTROY THE RESALE VALUE OF THIS DUSTBALL IF YOU KEEP MESSING IT UP.

"DRAGON BALLS."
THE ONE WHO KILLED RADITZ WILL KNOW WHERE THEY ARE.

GOOD POINT!
AND BEFORE WE SELL ANYTHING, WE'RE GOING TO FIND THOSE BALLS THAT'LL GET US A WISH GRANTED!

JUST SEARCH FOR THE HIGHEST POWER READING ON THIS PLANET...
HE'LL HAVE TO BE THE ONE WHO KILLED RADITZ. UNLESS IT'S KAKARROT'S SON...
BEEP

AND IF IT TURNS OUT ONE OF THOSE BALLS WAS AROUND HERE, WE MAY HAVE TO FORGET ABOUT OUR WISH FOR ETERNAL LIFE...
...ALL BECAUSE OF YOUR STUPID GREETING!
UGH! YOU'RE RIGHT! I WASN'T THINKING!

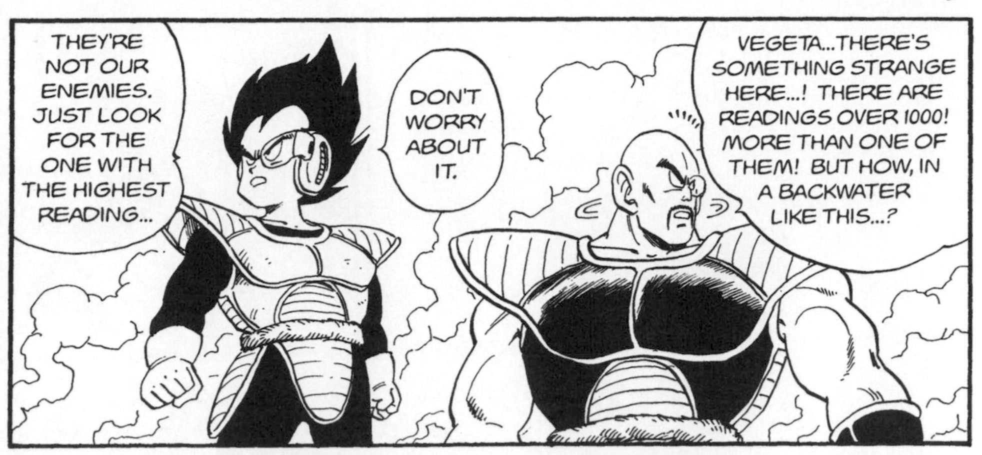

VEGETA...THERE'S SOMETHING STRANGE HERE...! THERE ARE READINGS OVER 1000! MORE THAN ONE OF THEM! BUT HOW, IN A BACKWATER LIKE THIS...?
DON'T WORRY ABOUT IT.
THEY'RE NOT OUR ENEMIES. JUST LOOK FOR THE ONE WITH THE HIGHEST READING...

—THERE! TWO HIGH READINGS...! AND CLOSE TO EACH OTHER...
LET'S GO, NAPPA...AND PAY OUR RESPECTS!

HO HO HO... THIS IS GREAT!

THE GRAVITY'S SO LOW, I FEEL LIKE I'M WEIGHTLESS!

!!
THEY'RE MOVING... !

THEY'RE HEADIN' STRAIGHT FOR THE OTHER TWO BIG CHI POWERS !!
IS IT TENSHINHAN AND CHAOZU... OR PICCOLO AND GOKU'S KID...?!

THE SAIYANS... THEY'RE COMING! STRAIGHT AT US!!
O-O-OKAY !!

CHAOZU ! YOU STAY BEHIND !
NO, I'M GOING TOO!! I TRAINED HARD FOR THIS!! I DESERVE TO GO!!

...REMAIN BAFFLED AT WHAT COULD TRIGGER AN EARTHQUAKE OF SUCH INCREDIBLE MAGNITUDE!
ALL CITIES NEAR THE EARTHQUAKE'S EPICENTER REMAIN INCOMMUNICADO, AS WORRIED FRIENDS AND FAMILY THROUGHOUT...

THEY'VE... THEY'VE FINALLY COME... !!

LET'S GO!! WE CAN LOCATE THEM WITH THIS!!
TH- THERE'S NOTHING *WE* CAN DO!!

I'M AFRAID HE'S RIGHT...
THEY ARE POWERFUL BEYOND OUR COMPREHENSION... WE'D ONLY GET IN THEIR WAY...ALL WE CAN DO FOR THEM...IS PRAY...
OH, YAMCHA... DON'T GET KILLED...!

SON GOKU...
WHERE *ARE* YOU... ?!

HOLD ON... I'M *COMING* !!
SHA SHA SHA---

12:20 PM...

SENSING THE IMPENDING VIOLENCE, THE BIRDS AND ANIMALS OF THE AREA BEGIN TO TAKE FLIGHT...

THERE'S NO NEED TO BE AFRAID...
WE'VE BECOME FAR STRONGER IN THIS ONE YEAR...
Y-YEAH! FAR!

!!
WHAT?! SOMETHING ELSE AP-PROACHING... FROM OVER THERE...!

AND STILL OTHERS... FROM ALL AROUND...!
AREN'T THERE S'POSED TO B-BE ONLY T-TWO?!

!
HSSS

TMP
S-SAIYAN ?!

HEY.
LONG TIME NO SEE, PICCOLO...

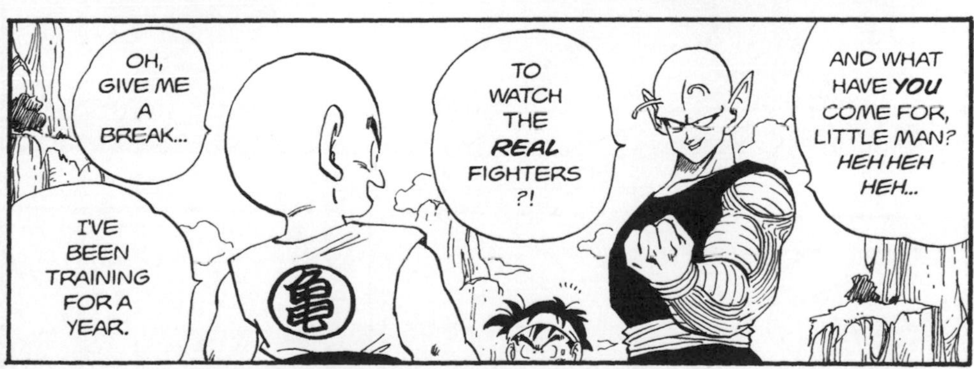
AND WHAT HAVE **YOU** COME FOR, LITTLE MAN? *HEH HEH HEH...*
TO WATCH THE ***REAL*** FIGHTERS ?!
OH, GIVE ME A BREAK...
I'VE BEEN TRAINING FOR A YEAR.

YOU SHOW SOME SLIGHT IMPROVEMENT, I'LL ADMIT...AND ARE THERE OTHER IDIOTS COMING TOO...?
ALL OF 'EM. I WAS JUST THE CLOSEST.

I REMEMBER YOU! FROM THE TURTLE GUY'S PLACE...

I'M KURIRIN.
AND YOU'RE LOOKING TOUGHER! LIKE WHEN GOKU WAS A KID!
YOU'RE SMALL BUT YOU'RE STRONG, HUH? MY DAD USED TO TELL ME ABOUT YOU!

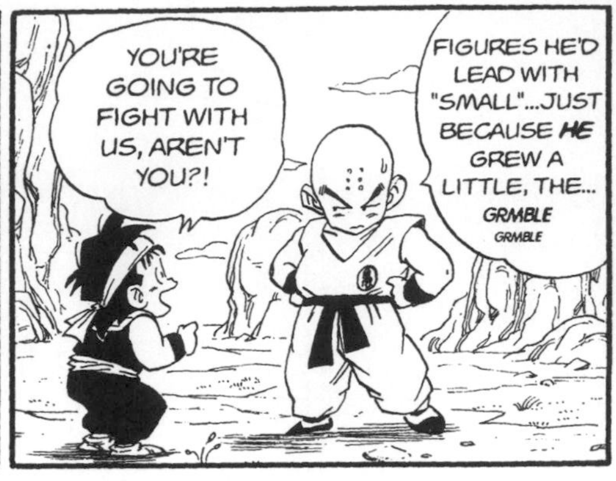
FIGURES HE'D LEAD WITH "SMALL"...JUST BECAUSE HE GREW A LITTLE, THE...
GRMBLE
GRMBLE
YOU'RE GOING TO FIGHT WITH US, AREN'T YOU?!

SO HOW BAD WAS IT, BEING TRAINED BY PICCOLO, OF ALL PEOPLE...?
HARD...
BUT HE WASN'T NEAR AS BAD AS EVERY-BODY—

THE SMALL TALK IS OVER.
THEY'RE HERE!!

!!

HEH HEH HEH... THERE THEY ARE...**THREE** MIGHTY SHRIMPS NOW...!
IT SEEMS THEY'VE BEEN EXPECTING US...

S-SO THOSE'RE THE SAIYANS, HUH...?!
MAN, I CAN FEEL THE CHI...L-LIKE A DEMONIC AURA...!

HAVE YOU BEEN PREPARING FOR US?

HOW DID YOU GUESS ?

DBZ:20 • Let the Games Begin!

AH, THAT VOICE...IT WAS *YOU* WHO KILLED RADITZ, WASN'T IT?

LET'S MAKE THIS CLEAR...
WHAT EXACTLY DO YOU WANT HERE...?!

VOICE... ?!

DIDN'T RADITZ TELL YOU ?
THIS ALSO SERVES AS A TRANS-MITTER.

HE'S A NAMEKIAN...
LOOKS LIKE IT...NOT SO STRANGE THAT RADITZ WAS BEATEN THEN...
?!

...NAMEKIAN...?

...PICCOLO... Y-YOU'RE AN ALIEN TOO...?! N-NO WONDER...
...
R-REALLY, PICCOLO ?

THEY SAY THESE SLIMY NAMEK GASTROPOD GUYS POSSESS STRANGE POWERS EVEN BEYOND THEIR EXTRAORDINARY FIGHTING ABILITIES... EVEN ***SORCERY***...
YOU'RE THE ONE WHO MADE THOSE DRAGON BALLS... AREN'T YOU?!

YOU...
YOU KNOW ABOUT THE DRAGON BALLS?!
WHY ELSE WOULD WE BOTHER WITH THIS DUMP?! HAND THEM OVER!
BRING ON ALL THE NAMEKIANS YOU CAN FIND! THEY'RE JUST **SLUGS** TO US!

HEH... THANKS TO YOU, I SUDDENLY HAVE A MUCH BETTER INSIGHT INTO MY ANCESTRY...

ALAS FOR ME, HOWEVER, I DID ***NOT*** MAKE THE DRAGON BALLS. MY SPECIALTY... IS COMBAT.

AS YOU WILL SEE.
NOW... ***WHO*** IS A SLUG ?!
SHK

SIR... ?
I NEVER DREAMED... THAT I WAS AN ALIEN...
I DID WONDER ABOUT THE ANTENNAE, OF COURSE...

IT'S ODD...WHEN I FIRST CREATED THE DRAGON BALLS, LONG AGO...I FELT CURIOUSLY NOSTALGIC...SOME SORT OF RACIAL MEMORY, I SUPPOSE...
PERHAPS ONE OF MY ANCESTORS ON THIS PLANET NAMEK HAD ONCE MADE SOMETHING MUCH LIKE THEM...

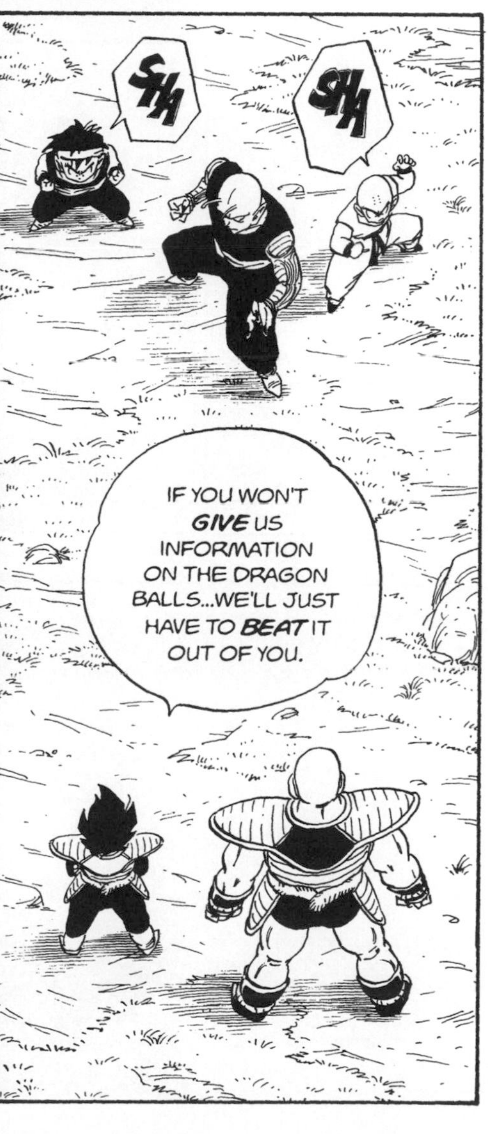
SHA
SHA
IF YOU WON'T GIVE US INFORMATION ON THE DRAGON BALLS...WE'LL JUST HAVE TO BEAT IT OUT OF YOU.

981... 1220... 1083...
BEEP BEEP BEEP
FOOLS! D'YOU THINK YOU CAN CHALLENGE US WITH POWER LEVELS LIKE THOSE?!

NAPPA, TAKE OFF YOUR SCOUTER.
WHAT ?

THESE SLUGS VARY THEIR POWERS TO SUIT THE BATTLE.
THOSE NUMBERS ARE WORTH-LESS.

YEAH...
THAT'S RIGHT...
POP
THAT WEAKLING RADITZ PROBABLY GOT HIMSELF ***KILLED*** BECAUSE HE DEPENDED ON THE SCOUTER'S NUMBERS AND GOT CAUGHT OFF GUARD.

"THAT..."
"THAT... WEAKLING..." ?

I-ISN'T RADITZ THE GUY WHO NEARLY CLOBBERED YOU AN' GOKU... ***TOGETHER***...?
...

"WEAKLING," HE SAYS...?
HEH HEH...

WHY DON'T WE SEE WHAT THEY CAN REALLY DO? THEN WE'LL ASK THEM ABOUT THE DRAGON BALLS AGAIN...
HEY, NAPPA... WEREN'T THERE SIX SEEDS FOR CULTIVARS LEFT?
HEH HEH HEH... YOU LIKE TO PLAY GAMES, DON'T YOU, VEGETA.

CULTIVARS...?
WH-WHAT ARE THOSE...?

FSH FSH!!

YEAH, THERE'S SIX, ALL RIGHT.

THEY'LL GROW WELL IN THIS SOIL.
POOSH POOSH

PIP PIP

SHK

plip plip

THERE...
fwip

WH-WHAT'S GOIN' ON...?

SPOP
SPOP SPOP

SPOPSPOP SPOP...!

!!

GRAUH...

YEEE--SH!
I-I DON'T LIKE THE LOOKS O' THOSE GUYS...!
THOSE THREE.
THEY ARE YOUR TARGETS.

TMP

TEN-SHINHAN! AND CHAOZU!

TMP
HUH ?!

SORRY I'M LATE !

YAMCHA !

THEY KEEP COMING, DON'T THEY?
LIKE A SWARM OF GNATS...

WEREN'T THERE SUPPOSED TO BE ***TWO*** SAIYANS?
MAYBE YOU SHOULD COM- PLAIN...
SIX OF THEM... THE SAME NUMBER AS THESE CULTIVARS... HOW PERFECT!
HOW ABOUT IF EACH OF YOU FIGHTS ONE AT A TIME?
FOR SPORT !

A GAME?! ABSURD!
QUIT PLAYING AND GET THIS OVER WITH!

NO! THIS COULD WORK FOR US!
GOKU'S NOT HERE YET...

FINE. I'LL GO FIRST.
COME AT ME.

I THINK THE CULTIVARS'LL SURPRISE THAT LITTLE MAN! *HA HA HA...!*
...

YOU TAKE THIS ONE.
GIVE HIM EVERY-THING.
T-TEN-SHINHAN! GOOD LUCK!

HYAH!

BAM

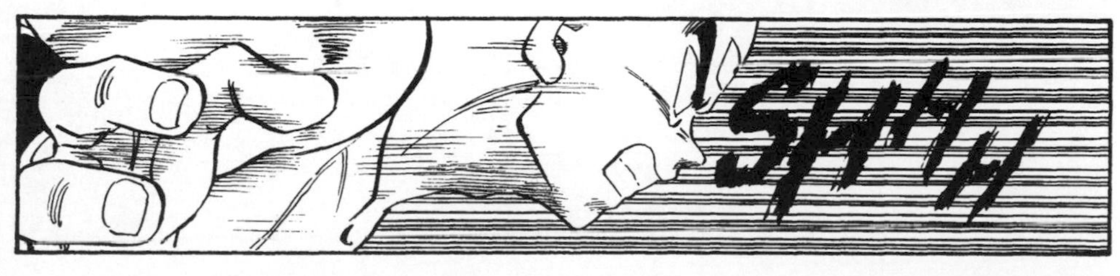

SSHHH
WAK !!!

BLISH

HSSS...
SSSS...
YEEK !!

HAAAAH!!!

DMM

DNSH

...!!
IT...IT CAN'T BE...!!

HE DID IT!
THAT'S TENSHINHAN FOR YOU!
PHEW.

HEH HEH HEH...
IT LOOKS LIKE THEY'LL BE ABLE TO ENTERTAIN US A LITTLE, AFTER ALL...

DBZ:21 • One Down...

g... guh... !

IT'S IMPOSSIBLE! THE CULTIVARS' POWER IS OVER 1200...!
EQUAL TO RADITZ, EVERY ONE OF THEM...!

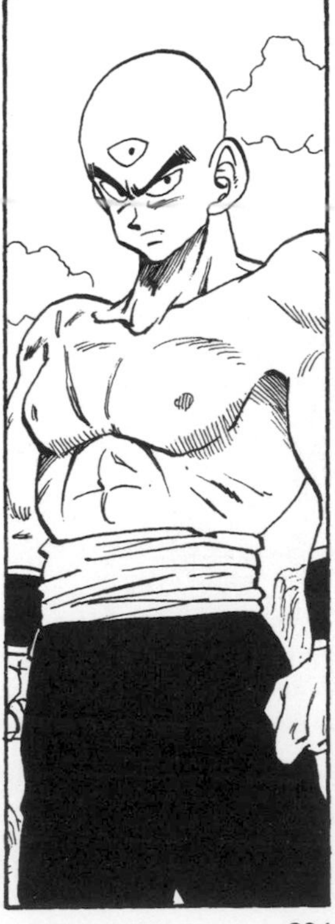

ERGO, THAT FELLOW'S POWER IS GREATER STILL.
BUT...
OUR DATA NEVER SHOWED THAT!

TENSHINHAN! HE'S GETTING BACK UP!

gruh...
!!

PSH

BOOM

BLICH

!!

WHA...
WHAT...?!

THE EARTHLING ALREADY HAD HIM BEATEN.
IT WOULD'VE BEEN A WASTE OF TIME.

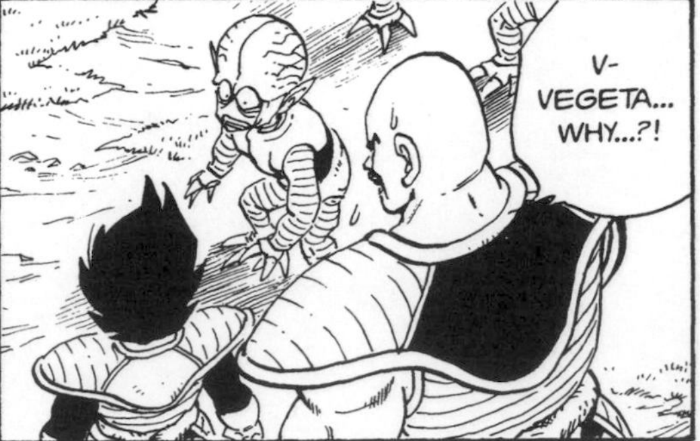
V-VEGETA... WHY...?!

YOUR COMRADE UNDER-ESTIMATED HIS FOE...
DIDN'T I TELL HIM TO GO ALL-OUT...?

OH...
M-M-MAN...

DESTROYED... WITH A GESTURE... WHAT POWER...!!

WHO'LL BE NEXT?
THIS TIME, HIT WITH EVERY-THING!!

O-OKAY...

LET ME DO IT.
I'LL TEACH THEM THAT PLAYTIME'S OVER.

LISTEN, YAMCHA, I CAN—
YOU'VE ALREADY BEEN RESTORED TO LIFE BY THE DRAGON BALLS. YOU DON'T GET ANOTHER CHANCE.

NOW *TRY* ME!

AH. A HOT-SHOT.
SHOW 'EM WHAT THE CULTIVARS ARE MADE OF!!
GUH!

HISSH

SHHH

FT
FT

THEY—
THEY'RE *GONE* !!

KAK

THEY'RE MOVING AT SUPER SPEED, IDIOT!! FEEL THEIR *CHI*!!
EVERYONE CAN SEE THEM BUT YOU!

DDDD

BBBB

GRAW
!!!!

!!

FT
!!

PFF

DM—…M

FWOO

...AGAIN...

TP

THESE MONSTERS AREN'T AS FEARSOME AS THEY LOOK.
I'LL CLEAN UP THE OTHER FOUR BY MYSELF...

PK...

HEH HEH...
SEEMS IT'S YOUR TURN TO UNDER-ESTIMATE...

WHAT ?!

GOMP
!!

YAA!!!

HNN...

KRAK

heh
NOW THAT...IS MORE LIKE IT.

I-IT JUST...
IT SELF-DESTRUCTED...

YAMCHA !!

...

...HE'S
DEAD...

H-HE KNEW THIS
WAS GOING TO
HAPPEN...THAT'S
WHY HE WOULDN'T
LET ME DO IT...
HOW AM I
GONNA BREAK
THIS...TO PU'AR
AND BULMA...?!

SETTLING
FOR A
DRAW?!!
THIS IS
PATHETIC
!!!
PICK
UP YOUR
TRASH,
LITTLE
MAN!

...!
SHUT...
YOUR...
MOUTH
!!

GET
BACK,
ALL OF
YOU!

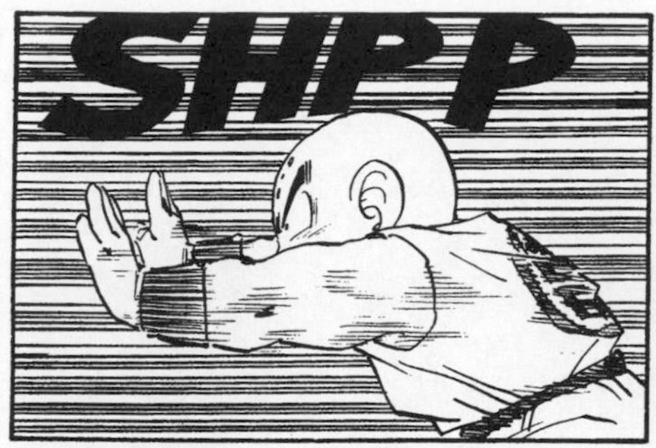
SHPP

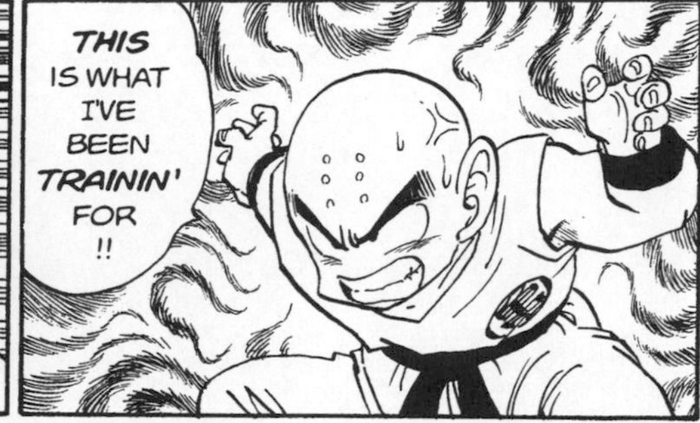
THIS IS WHAT I'VE BEEN TRAININ' FOR !!

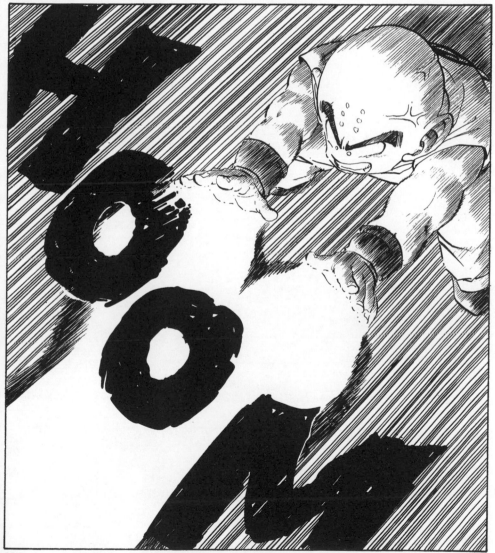

HYOO

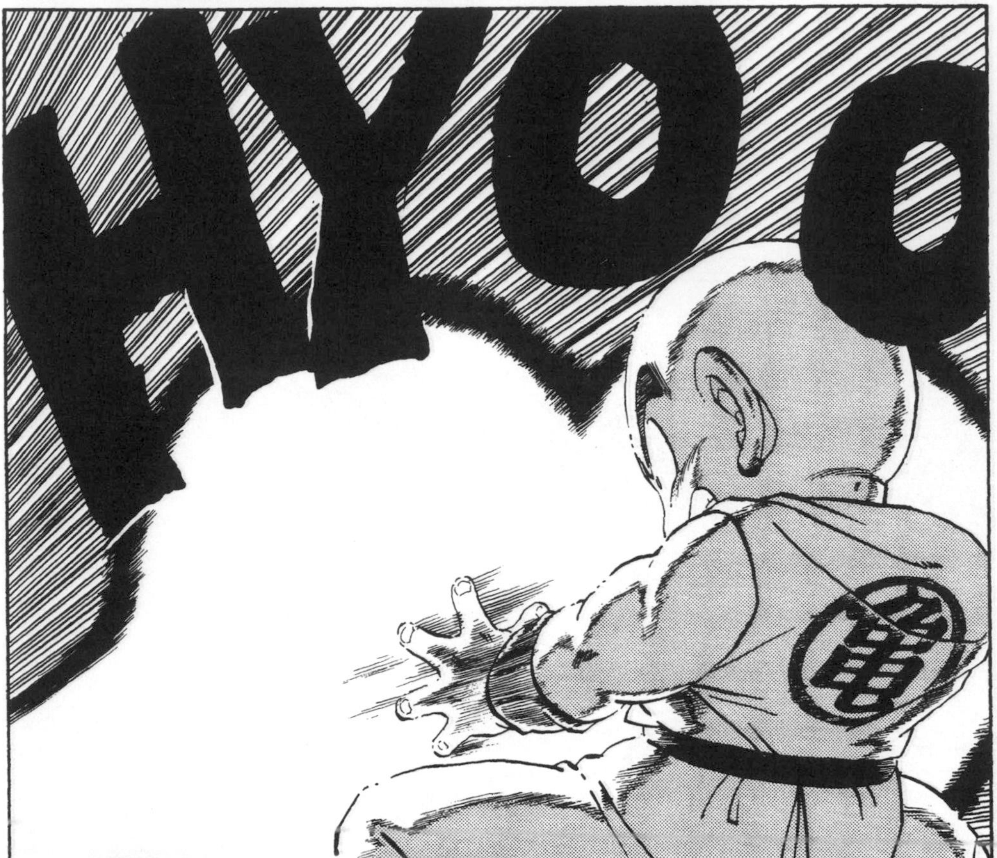

VWOOOO

CHAOZU, GET BACK !!!
IT'LL BLOW YOU TO PIECES !!!!

TREMEN-DOUS POWER— BUT NO SPEED !!
IT'S LIKE A SIGN SAYING, "GET AWAY"!!

BA
BA
BA

heh

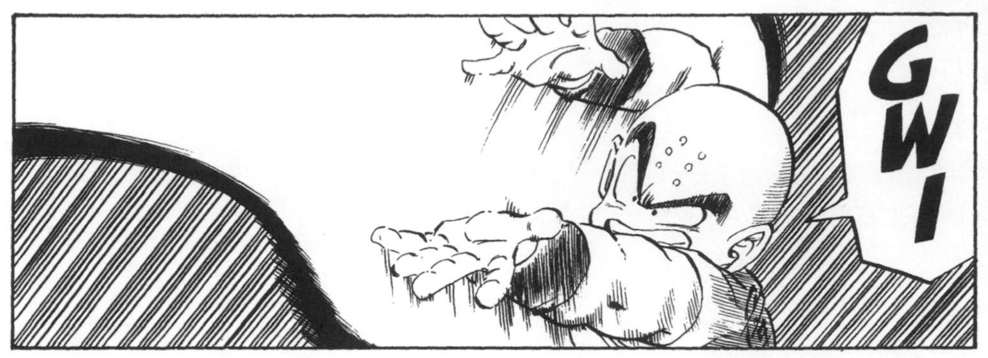
GWI

HAA!!!!

HYUU

GNN

BAFF

DOOM
DOOM
DOOM
DOOM

DOOM DOOM

RRMMMM...

HE DID IT !!

huff huff
HEH HEH... I MISSED ONE...

WOW...
WOW, KURIRIN!!

BWOM

!!

IT'S THE ONE HE MISSED !!!

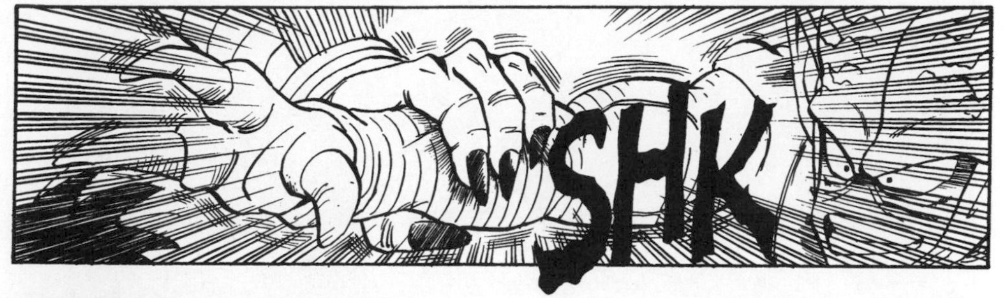

gg... !!

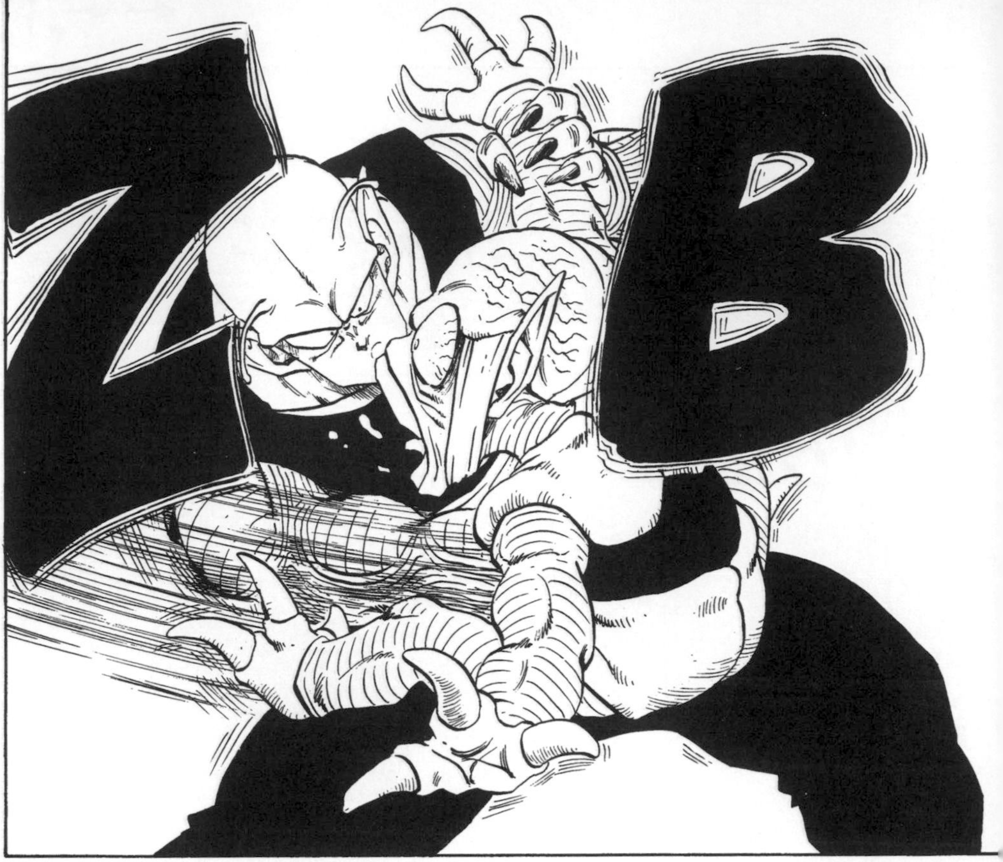

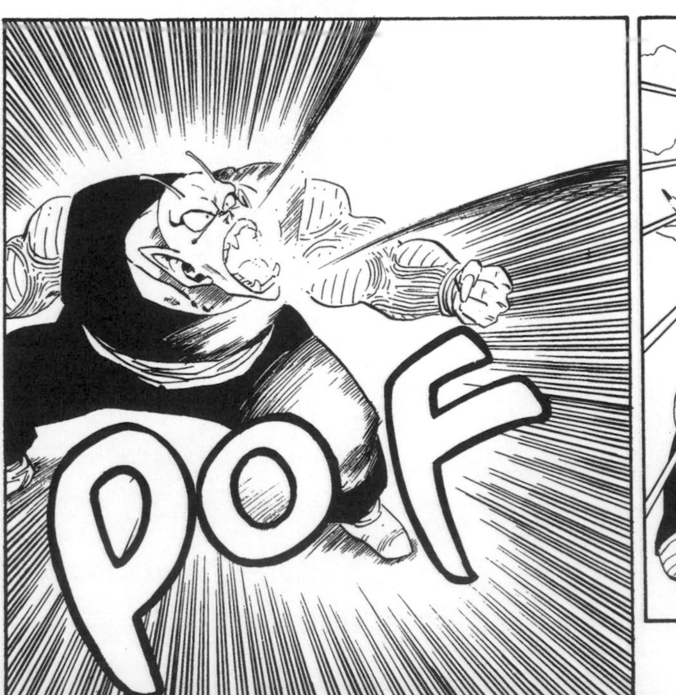
POF

VNN

WELL... THAT'S PICCOLO...

ENJOY IT...'TIL HE'S OUR ENEMY AGAIN...

HOO BOY...

TH-THANK YOU, PICCOLO...

DON'T MISUNDERSTAND.

I WOULDN'T BOTHER SAVING YOU...

...EXCEPT THAT I NEEDED A LITTLE WARM-UP FOR THE GREAT BATTLE TO COME...

HEH HEH HEH...
I HOPE IT **WILL** BE A GREAT BATTLE...

!!

ERK...!

ACK...!

YOU **DID** SAY YOU WANTED PLAYTIME TO END, DIDN'T YOU?
HAW HAW... NOW IT'S TIME FOR THE REAL THING.

IT'S NOT POSSIBLE... IT DIDN'T AFFECT THEM AT ALL...!
THEY... THEY MUST HAVE TAKEN IT HEAD-ON...

B-BUT I... I USED MY FULL POWER!!!
SO THIS... IS WHAT SAIYANS ARE...!!

LET ME DO IT. I'LL KILL ALL FIVE AT ONCE.
...AS YOU WILL.

HEH HEH HEH...
THANKS FOR LETTING ME HAVE THE FUN...

HYA-AAA...
RMMM
TH... THE EARTH... !!!
...THE EARTH'S SHAKING... !!!
T-TEN-SHINHAN !!!
MY POWERS DON'T WORK !!!
NO... IT CAN'T BE... !!!!
PICCOLO... HELP... !!!
I NEVER THOUGHT... IT WOULD BE SO MUCH... !!!!

VSHH

...

GLMP

HERE IT COMES... !!!!!

P-POP-POP

HOO BOY...

DragonBallZ

VOLUME 3

EARTH VS. THE SAIYANS

WHO DO I KILL FIRST?!

OKAY...

DBZ:23 • Hope Runs Out

HYAAAH !!

NOW !!!!!

HIYAAA
DROP!!!!

SSH
!!
AAUGH
!!!
TENSHINHAN!!
HEH... BREAK-ABLE.

NEXT !!!

YOU...

SCUM !!!

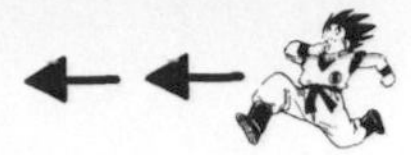

HAH!!

ZUUNG

AA
!!!

GBOOM

BLACH
NO—!!!!
NNN... GUH..... !!
STUBBORN VERMIN.
HE JUST WON'T DIE.
AH... AH... AH... AH..... !
WHAT... **POWER!!**

PWI--

BWOOOM

AUGH
!!!

huff huff
huff huff

CAN'T SEE... THE BOTTOM...
NEVER DREAMED... SUCH A BLAST...!

CH-CHAOZU...?!
!!

WHERE *IS* HE?!
IF HE WAS CAUGHT IN THAT—!!

WH...
WHAT...?!!

NAPPA!
BEHIND YOU!

HUH?

BLAP
HEY !!!!

CHAOZU !!!!

!!

UNKH !
TH- THIS LITTLE... !!

WHAT ARE YOU TRYING TO DO... ?!!
GET OUT OF THERE !!

GOODBYE, TENSHINHAN...
SAVE YOUR-SELF.

Y-YOU CAN'T...

NO... WAIT...

CHAOZU !!!!

DON'T !!!!

DOOM

RRR--M

CHAOZU !!!!

...CH...
...CHAOZU...

SO...BLEW HIMSELF UP TO TAKE OUT AN OPPONENT...
HE'S WON MY RESPECT...
AA... AAAA...

HEH HEH HEH... WHAT A WASTE...
YOU STILL JUST DON'T **GET** IT, DO YOU...?

SHHH
SH SHSH

IT'S TAKING TOO LONG... !!!
BLAST IT... !!!
GOTTA GO !!!!
GO !!!!
VWOOO

CHAOZU GAVE HIS LIFE...FOR NOTHIN'...!!
'S-S-SNOT POSSIBLE...! I-IT DIDN'T EVEN...FAZE 'IM...!

THE DRAGON BALLS... ALREADY RESTORED HIS LIFE ONCE...
HE CAN NEVER COME BACK... EVER AGAIN...!!

DON'T WORRY... *HEH*... YOU'LL ALL GET YOUR TURN..... !!
ALL RIGHT... FIRST THREE-EYES... THEN THE RUNT!

LISTEN...IN THE INSTANT HE MOVES TO ATTACK...HE'S OPEN...
WE'LL USE THAT INSTANT...

GOOD PLAN.
I HOPE IT WORKS.

...

SO CONFI-DENT...
I HOPE TO SEE YOUR FACE WHEN SON GOKU ARRIVES...

DON'T LOOK AT ME. YOU'LL MISS YOUR INSTANT.

LUCKILY, YOU'LL SEE HIM SOON—*IN HELL* !!
YOU'LL *PAY* FOR THIS... !!!!

OH ?
AND WHO'S THAT? YOUR SECRET WEAPON?

HYAAAH~!!!!

!!

NOW !!!!

GO !!!!

SHHK
SHHK

COME AT ME... !!!!

NOW DIE !!!!!
!!

WHAT ?!!

PWIK

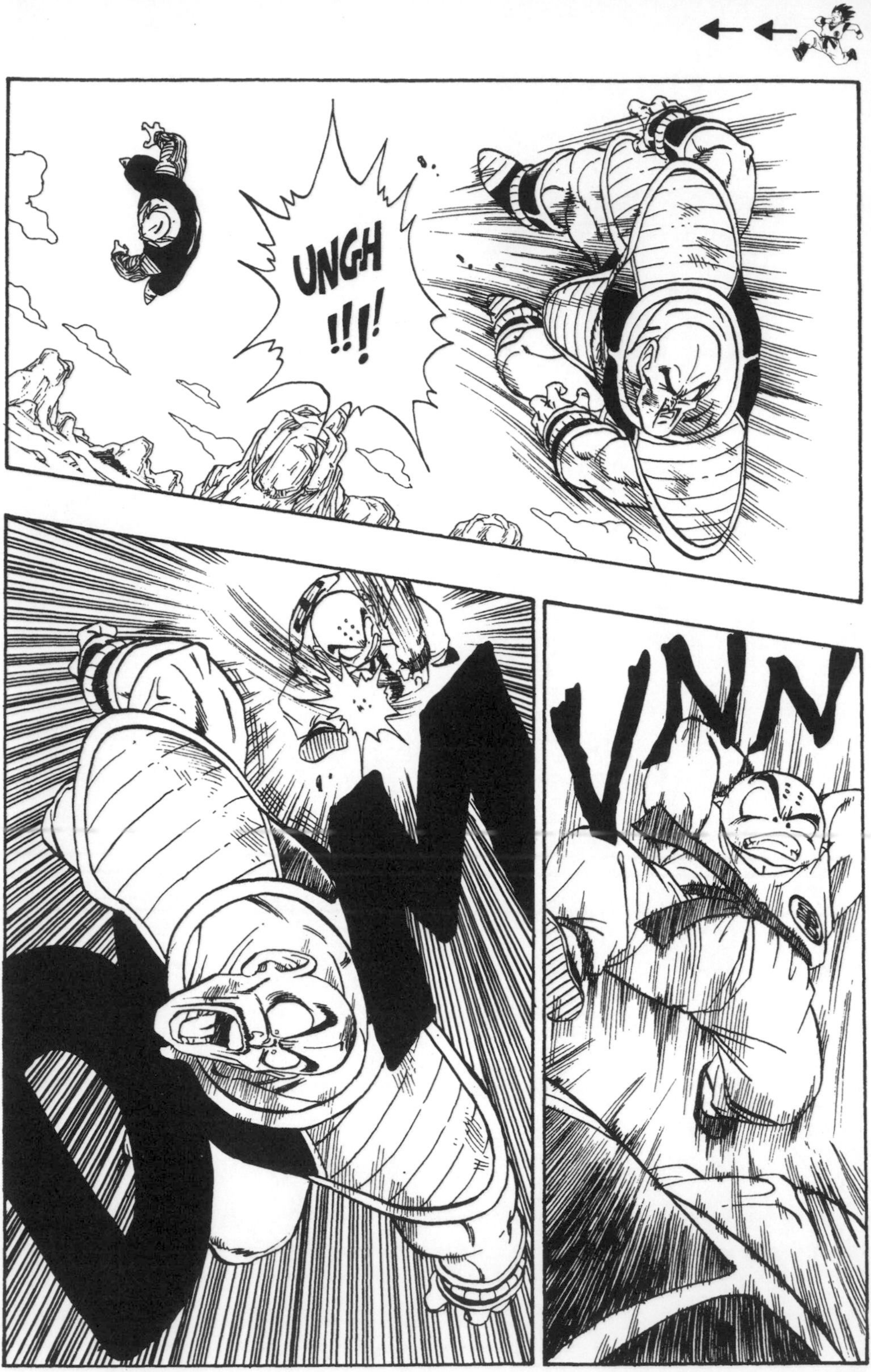

UNGH !!!!

VNN

GOHAN, NOW !!!!!
FIRE !!!!
UH...
UHHH... !!
!!
GO-HAN !!!!!

B-BUT...
I'M SCARED.....!!!!
.....!!
COWARD!!!
WE GOTTA DO IT!!!!!
RRAH!!!!!
HYOOOM

NGH !!!!
HE DODGED IT !!!!
WE WERE TOO LATE... !!!!
UH !!!!
HAH !!!!

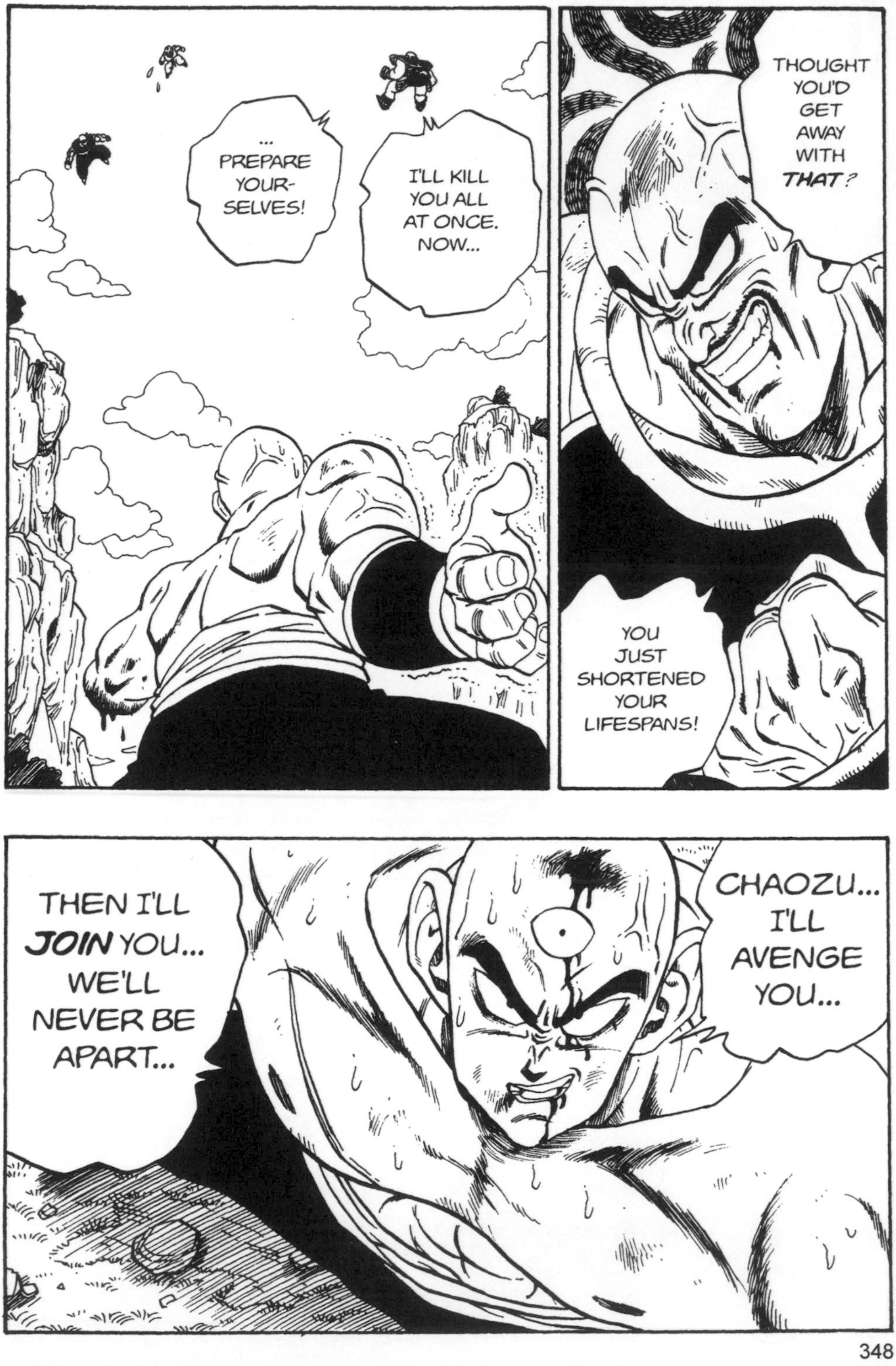

THOUGHT YOU'D GET AWAY WITH ***THAT?***
YOU JUST SHORTENED YOUR LIFESPANS!

I'LL KILL YOU ALL AT ONCE. NOW...

... PREPARE YOUR-SELVES!

CHAOZU... I'LL AVENGE YOU...
THEN I'LL ***JOIN*** YOU... WE'LL NEVER BE APART...

KI KŌ HŌ!!!!!

* "KI CANNON", OR "CHI KUNG PAO"

?!

!!
WHHM
AAARRR

......

PHEW...
DON'T SCARE ME LIKE THAT!

HE'S... A MONSTER...

I...
...I FAILED...
GWAA!

DMM...

HE FOUGHT LIKE A MAN... AND DIED LIKE A DOG...

GO-KUUU !!!!
HURRY !!!!

IM... POS-SIBLE...
IS HE... IMMORTAL... ?!

AH..... AH.....

..... !!

DBZ:25 • Goku, Hurry!

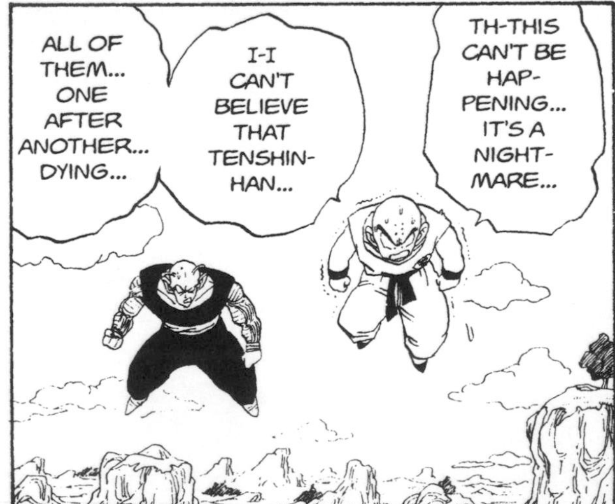
TH-THIS CAN'T BE HAP-PENING... IT'S A NIGHT-MARE...
I-I CAN'T BELIEVE THAT TENSHIN-HAN...
ALL OF THEM... ONE AFTER ANOTHER... DYING...

GOKU!!!! GET HERE!!!!
PLEE-EASE!!!!

HEH... ANOTHER ONE DOWN...
NOW IT'S YOUR TURN...

ALTHOUGH I'LL LET THAT NAMEK CALLED PICCOLO LIVE...MORE OR LESS...
...SO HE CAN TELL US MORE ABOUT THE DRAGON BALLS...

"GOKU"...? THIS ISN'T THE FIRST TIME THEY'VE...
...WAIT...

LUCKY YOU, PICCOLO...THEY THINK YOU'RE THE ONLY ONE WHO KNOWS ABOUT THE DRAGON BALLS...
IT WON'T MATTER...
THEY PLAN TO KILL US ALL ANYWAY...

BUT LISTEN... I'M GLAD YOU'RE ON OUR SIDE, EVEN IF IT'S TEMPORARY...
I NEVER THOUGHT THIS'D HAPPEN...

SO HOW MUCH CONFIDENCE D'YOU HAVE THAT YOU'LL WIN...?
NONE!

I NEVER DREAMED THERE WAS SUCH POWER...
THEY FAR OUTSTRIP THE SAIYAN WHO CAME BEFORE...

THEN... I GUESS...
THIS IS REALLY IT...

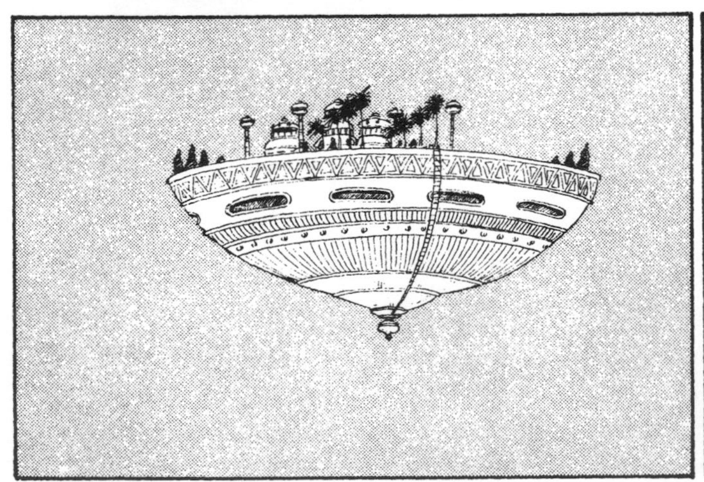

WHAT COULD HE BE DOING... ?!
HOW CAN HE NOT BE HERE ALREADY?
HURRY, SON GOKU!

YOU DO NOT FEEL HIS PRESENCE?
NO...
I FEEL ONLY...THAT I HAVE LITTLE TIME LEFT...
THAT DEATH IS VERY NEAR...

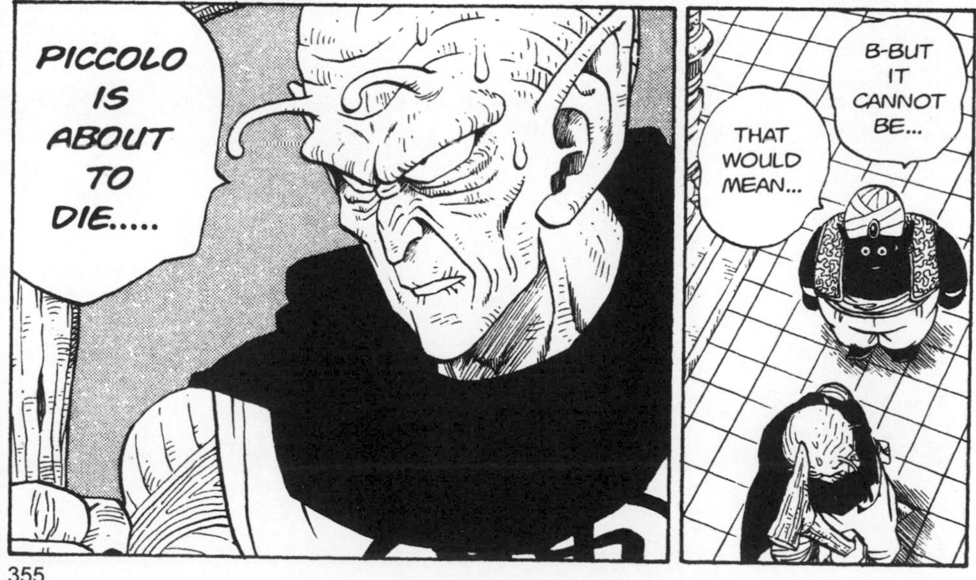
B-BUT IT CANNOT BE...
THAT WOULD MEAN...
PICCOLO IS ABOUT TO DIE.....

WHEREVER YOU WANT...
HEH...
IT'LL BE THE SAME RESULT !

WE HAVE TO FIGHT HIM ON THE GROUND !
HE'S TOO ACCUSTOMED TO AERIAL COMBAT!

HYUN
HYUN

TM
TM

HYAAAH!

DADDY...
!!

NOW!!!!!

NAPPA, WAIT !!!!!

!!

?!

WHAT'S WRONG WITH YOU, VEGETA?!
ALL I HAVE TO DO IS...

...?!

DON'T BE IN SUCH A HURRY, THAT'S ALL.
I WANT TO ASK THEM SOME-THING.

LIKE WHAT ?!

...

THIS "SON GOKU" YOU KEEP MENTIONING IS KAKARROT... ISN'T HE?
AM I RIGHT?

YEAH!
SO WHAT?!

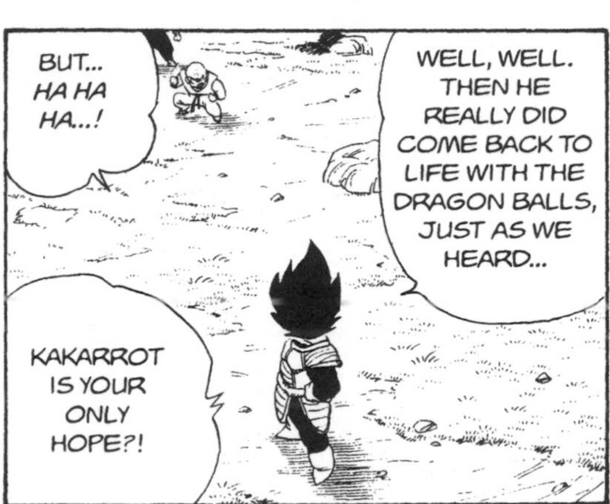
WELL, WELL. THEN HE REALLY DID COME BACK TO LIFE WITH THE DRAGON BALLS, JUST AS WE HEARD...
BUT... *HA HA HA...!*
KAKARROT IS YOUR ONLY HOPE?!

WHAT GOOD WILL HE BE IF HE WASN'T EVEN A MATCH FOR RADITZ?

HE SHOULD BE DIFFERENT FROM BEFORE...NO!! HE ***WILL*** BE DIFFERENT!!
MORE POWERFUL THAN ***EVER BEFORE*** !!!

SON GOKU IS A BAD ONE TO UNDER-ESTIMATE!

WA HA HA!
THEN WHERE *IS* HE?!
MAYBE HE'S NOT COMING BACK... BECAUSE HE'S *AFRAID*!!
AH..... !!

HE'LL COME!! DADDY'LL COME BACK!! AND HE'LL BEAT YOU GUYS UP!!

HEH HEH...
SUCH FAITH...

TOUCHING.
ALL RIGHT, THEN. WE'LL WAIT UNTIL HE COMES.

WHAT?! VEGETA, YOU'RE JOKING!
HE'S NEVER GOING TO COME!
LET'S JUST FINISH THEM OFF *NOW*!

WE'LL WAIT FOR THREE HOURS.
AND NO LONGER.

THREE HOURS !!!
WHAT AM I SUPPOSED TO DO FOR THREE HOURS?! I'VE BEEN IN SUSPENDED ANIMATION FOR TOO LONG!!
MY BODY IS HUNGRY FOR ACTION!!
FORGET WAITING !!!

NAPPA !!!!
DO WHAT I SAY !!!!

S...
SORRY...
I...GOT CARRIED AWAY...

WELL, THERE YOU GO.
THREE EXTRA HOURS OF LIFE. ENJOY THEM.

I'M...I'M SORRY...BUT I GOT SO S-SCARED...

AWAY WITH YOU, THEN! WE HAVE NO USE FOR A COWARD.
I WAS A FOOL TO EXPECT SO MUCH.
HEY, COME ON... IT'S HIS FIRST FIGHT...

THE WAY THE BIG ONE COWERED... THAT MUST MEAN...
...THAT THE LITTLE ONE IS EVEN MORE POWERFUL...
IT'S HOPE-LESS!

I STILL DON'T GET IT...WHY DO WE WANT TO WAIT FOR KAKARROT?
BECAUSE HE'S A TRAITOR TO ALL SAIYANS.
A TRAITOR DESERVES TO SEE HIS SON AND FRIENDS DIE BEFORE HIS EYES...
DESERVES TO FEEL HOW POWERLESS HE IS...HOW MUCH AGONY WE CAN INFLICT...
UNTIL, AFTER THREE OR FOUR HOURS...*HEH*... HE'LL BEG US TO SEND HIM TO HELL.

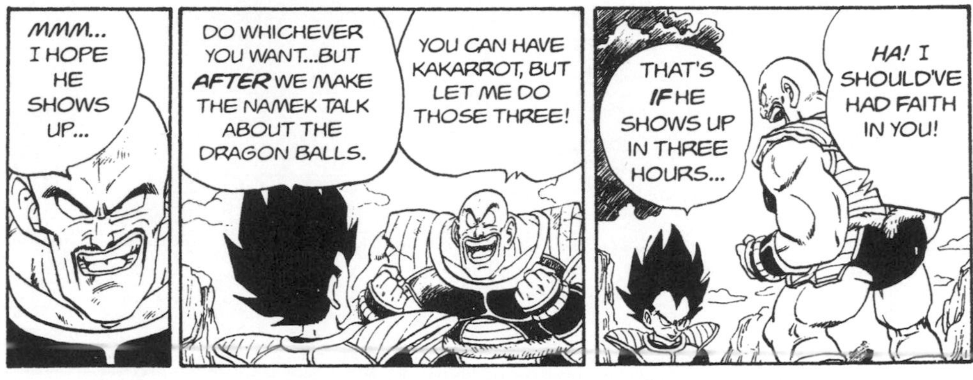
HA! I SHOULD'VE HAD FAITH IN YOU!
THAT'S *IF* HE SHOWS UP IN THREE HOURS...
YOU CAN HAVE KAKARROT, BUT LET ME DO THOSE THREE!
DO WHICHEVER YOU WANT...BUT ***AFTER*** WE MAKE THE NAMEK TALK ABOUT THE DRAGON BALLS.
MMM... I HOPE HE SHOWS UP...

WHAT'S ***KEEPING*** HIM...?!
DID HE REALLY EVEN COME BACK TO ***LIFE***...?!

WHY DON'T WE JUST RUN AWAY?!
WHY JUST STAND HERE AND ***DIE***?!

FOOL...THEY'RE PLANNING TO ANNIHILATE MANKIND ANYWAY...
DO YOU PREFER TO DIE RUNNING OR STANDING?

RRRRG... PLEASE, GOKU...COME QUICK...!
AND BE MORE POWERFUL THAN THEM... PLEASE !!

WHERE IS HE... ?!!

SLOWLY... AGONIZINGLY... THREE HOURS CRAWL PAST...

IT'S TIME...
IT SEEMS WE'VE BEEN STOOD UP...
PIPP

DBZ:26 • Back from the Other Side

WITHOUT SON GOKU, WE HAVE ONE LAST CHANCE...
ALTHOUGH IT'S A LONG SHOT...

LISTEN CLEARLY... KURIRIN, WAS IT? YOU DRAW HIS ATTENTION...

WHILE I GO FOR THE SAIYANS' ONLY WEAKNESS... THE TAIL...
...OH YEAH... !

ONCE I HAVE HIM POWERLESS... THEN, GOHAN, YOU STRIKE WITH ALL YOU'VE GOT! UNDERSTAND...?
Y-YEAH... !

TH-THIS TIME I WON'T RUN AWAY...I PR-PROMISE... !

SEE THAT YOU DON'T !
CONSIDER EARTH'S FATE TO BE IN YOUR HANDS...

WHOA... THAT'S PICCOLO, ALL RIGHT...
I ACTUALLY HAVE HOPE... I THINK WE CAN WIN...!

BE CONFIDENT, GOHAN...IF YOU PUT YOUR MIND TO IT, YOUR POWER SURPASSES MINE...

B-BUMP B-BUMP
B-BUMP B-BUMP

HYUUUUU...

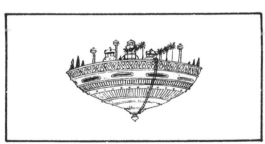

HEH...

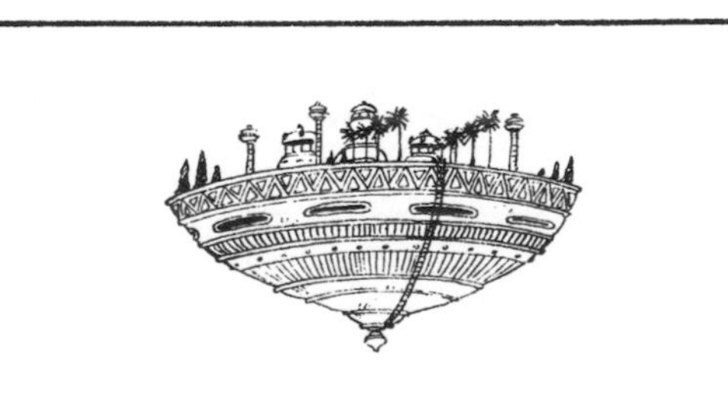

!!

—IT'S SON GOKU!!!
HE'S CLOSE!!!
FETCH HIM, MY LORD! HURRY!

HSSH

I SEE IT!!!!
THE END OF THE ROAD!!!!

HWA
huff
huff

UNBE-LIEVABLE!!!
SUCH SPEED!!!

TUMP

GOKU !!!
KAMI-SAMA !!!

TAKE HOLD—HURRY !!!
THANKS !!!
THE HON. EN

VIZZZ

TH- THAT MORTAL...
...ACTUALLY RETURNED FROM KAIŌ-SAMA, THE LORD OF WORLDS...
WHO'S WHO
THE HON. ENMA

PFFT

THE TRAINING WENT WELL !!
huff
NOW, I'M OFF !!
huff
YOU'RE OUR ONLY HOPE!!
GOOD LUCK, SON GOKU!!

GYOW

BNG

EVERYONE...
GOHAN...
PLEASE BE ALIVE...!!
KIIII...N

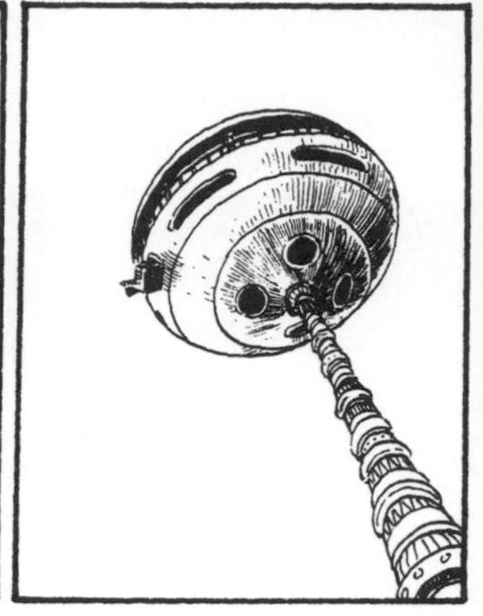

HERE HE COMES!
ALTHOUGH HE LOOKS AWFULLY TIRED...!

HELLO!!!

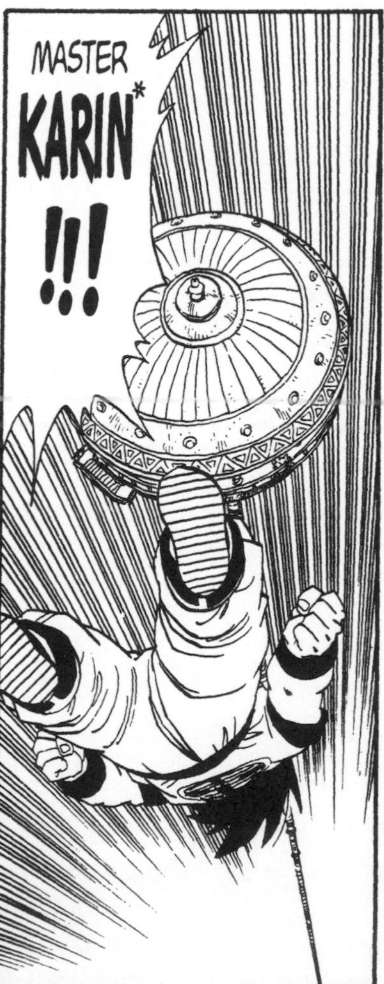

MASTER KARIN*!!!

HERE ARE THE LAST TWO SENZU BEANS!! TAKE THEM!!!

THANKS!!!
DOK
DOK

I NEEDED THESE!!
WE'RE COUNTING ON YOU!!!

*IT'S A LONG STORY...SEE **DRAGON BALL**, VOLUME 8!

I'LL EAT ONE NOW...
MNNG MNNG...

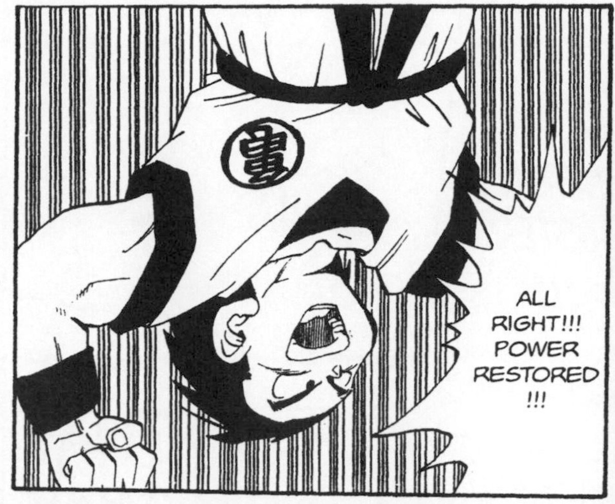

ALL RIGHT!!! POWER RESTORED !!!

KINTO-UUUUN !!!!

IT'S BEEN A WHILE!!! COME ON!!!!
VOO---N

ffp

A HUGE **ENERGY CLUSTER** !!!

THAT WAY !!!!

ZHOOOOM

OKAY !!!!
HERE GOES !!!!

BWA
RRRAAH !!!!

EAGER FOR *DEATH,* ARE YOU?!

THEY MUST HAVE A PLAN.

GULP...

DRAW HIS ATTENTION... !!!

VSHH!

GNG
Pfi
!!

GO-
HAA----N
!!!!

WAAA
AAAAH
!!!!

WE DID IT!!

FOOLS!!

HUH?!

.....

GUH
!!!!!

KI
!!

HEY! DON'T DIE YET!
FMMP
WE STILL HAVE TO ASK YOU ABOUT THE DRAGON BALLS... *HEH HEH HEH...*

IT... CAN... NOT... BE...

WHAT FOOLS DO YOU TAKE US FOR?!
DID YOU THINK WE WOULDN'T PROTECT AGAINST SUCH A *WEAKNESS* ?!

N...NO... PLEASE... NO...

DISAPPOINTING... NOT EVEN THE BEST ON THIS PLANET CAN MAKE IT PAST THE FIRST BLOW...
HEH HEH HEH...
DM!

THE WEAKNESS OF THE SAIYANS HAS ALWAYS BEEN THEIR TAILS...BUT AS PICCOLO HAS JUST DISCOVERED, THESE TWO HAVE OVERCOME EVEN THAT. HE THOUGHT HE'D ALREADY FOUGHT THE GREATEST POWERS THE COSMOS HAD TO OFFER...BUT NOW...

DBZ:27 • The Time Draws Near

IT'S... IT'S OVER...
WELL...IF HE'S GONNA TAKE A NAP...I GUESS I HAVE TO PLAY WITH HIS LITTLE FRIENDS...HEH HEH HEH...

HEH... WHAT A FATHER YOU'VE GOT...
LEAVING HIS LITTLE BOY...TO *DIE*...

COME ON! YOU'RE KAKARROT'S SON. YOU'VE GOT SAIYAN BLOOD IN YOU TOO. YOU CAN GIVE ME A REAL FIGHT, CAN'T YA?

NO...
DON'T... !

SSSS

WOKK

UFF !!

DMMM

...!!

HEY, DON'T DIE YET! I WANT TO PLAY!

...N...
...HN.....

hakk

HUHH HUHH
HUHH

THERE YOU GO...!
FIGHT LIKE A SAIYAN !

AND DIE LIKE ONE !!!

TAKE THAT!!!
!!
DOOOM

ZZZZZZ

!!

GNG

VNNN
FSSH

VSHH
VRRRRRR
STMP

AUGH !!!
GNG

HM !
HE CAN MOVE, AT LEAST.

STAND STILL...
AND **FIGHT** !!!
DOMP

SH

*"CIRCLE OF CHI"

HAH
!

GWURRRRRR

PARLOR
TRICKS
!

ZZAM

USE YOUR HEAD, IDIOT!

MISSED...!

YOU... LITTLE... DUNG-BALL! YOU CUT ME...!
UH-OH...

I'M REALLY GONNA LIKE THIS !!!!!

!!

EEP!!
HWAA

POK
EEE-YAA!!!

HEH
ONE MORE BLOW !!!!
ZNN
DM

?!!

SMP

AAAARH...!!!

IT CAN'T BE... !!!
YOU'RE TOUGHER THAN YOU LOOK...!!

huff
huff

THE *EARTH*...
...DOESN'T GO DOWN EASILY... !!

BWAA HA HA! HAVING TROUBLE, NAPPA ?

YOU STUPID FREAK !!

NOW YOU'VE MADE ME MAD!!

I TOOK IT EASY ON YOU BECAUSE WE WANT YOU TO TELL US WHERE THOSE DRAGON BALLS ARE!! BUT ***NOW***...!!!

DBZ:28 • The Death of a God!!

IT'S **SON GOKU**!!! HE'S **COMING**!!!

I SHOULD HAVE KNOWN THAT FOOL WOULD MAKE US WAIT!!!

DADDY... DADDY'S COMING...!!!
HURRY!! HURRY!!!

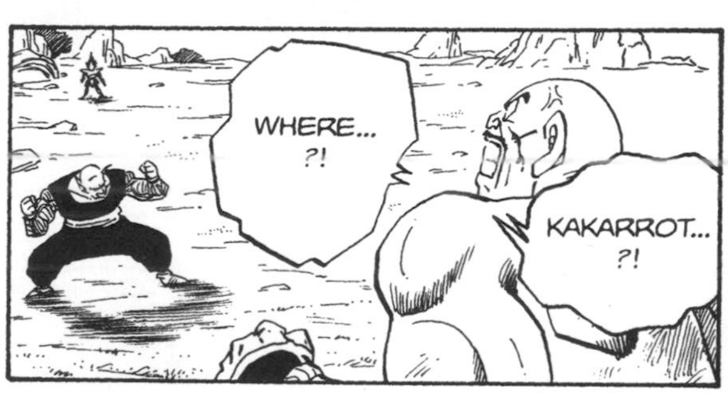

WHERE...?!
KAKARROT...?!

THEY SEEM TO HAVE THE POWER...
TO DETECT CHI?
PI
LET'S SEE...

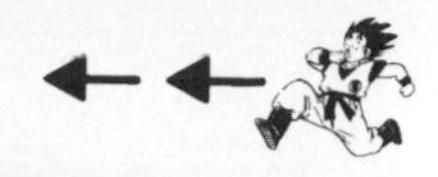

HWOO

TWO **BIG** CHI POWERS... TWO EVEN **BIGGER**... AND ONE **SMALL**...
!!

IT'S NOT **ENOUGH**...!!
PLEASE... DON'T LET ANYONE BE **DEAD**...
!!

HOOW

FASTER, KINTO'UN...

FLY FASTER !!!!

!!

VEGETA! ARE THEY TELLING THE TRUTH?!
I *HOPE* THEY ARE... *HEH HEH HEH...!!*

I DON'T KNOW IF IT'S REALLY KAKARROT...
BUT HE'LL BE HERE IN FOUR MINUTES...

WITH A POWER LEVEL...
OF 5,000!!

...5,000?!

TH...THAT'S IMPOSSIBLE!
I-IT HAS TO BE A MISTAKE...

IT MAY BE. THESE FOOLS SEEM ABLE TO VARY THEIR POWER. MEANING... 5,000 COULD BE JUST FOR STARTERS...

HEH...I DO BELIEVE YOUR PARTNER'S ACTUALLY WORRIED !!

NAPPA!! KILL THOSE TWO NOW !!!
THEIR HELP COULD ACTUALLY MAKE KAKARROT A CHALLENGE...
...BUT THEIR CORPSES MIGHT WELL SHAKE HIM UP!!

WHAT?!

!!

B-BUT THE DRAGON BALLS... HOW'LL WE FIND...?!
NEVER MIND THAT! WE DON'T NEED THEM!!

I NEVER BELIEVED THE LEGEND OF THE NAMEKIAN POWER SPHERES...BUT IF KAKARROT'S REALLY RETURNED FROM THE DEAD, THEN IT'S TRUE!!
THAT MEANS THERE MUST BE MORE BALLS ON THIS FOOL'S HOME PLANET. A LITTLE RAMPAGE THROUGH NAMEK WOULD BE A LOVELY WAY TO WIND DOWN AFTER THE DESTRUCTION OF EARTH, HMM?

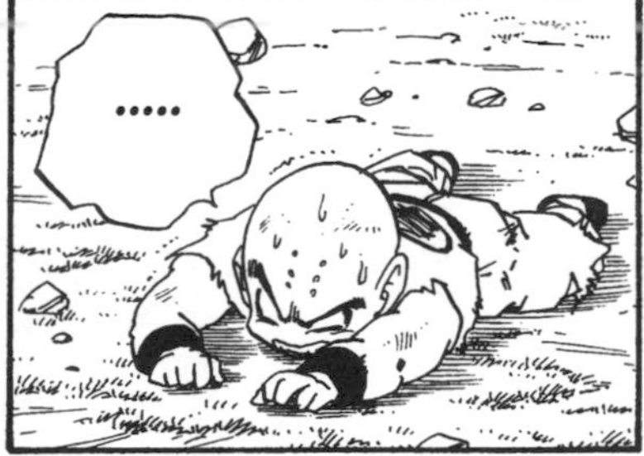
......

I STILL SAY YOUR MACHINE'S BROKEN... KAKARROT CAN'T BE ANY 5,000...
...BUT IT'S A GOOD ENOUGH EXCUSE TO START THE KILLING...

......

PICCOLO, YOU'VE GOT TO **RUN**!!!
I'LL HOLD 'EM OFF SOMEHOW 'TIL DADDY COMES !!
IF YOU DIE, THEN THE EARTH-GOD KAMI-SAMA WILL DIE... AND THEN THE DRAGON BALLS WILL BE GONE!!

FEH...
DON'T BE RIDICULOUS, BOY. YOU CAN'T HOLD THEM OFF ALONE...

S... SOME-THING REALLY BAD...IS ABOUT TO HAPPEN...
AN' I CAN'T... MOVE... CAN'T STOP IT...
SO... THE LITTLE LAD'S GOING TO HOLD ME OFF, EH?

DON'T MAKE ME **LAUGH** !!!!

GOHAN !!!!
!!
WA HA HA HA HA !!!
HST
HYAAA!!!!!!

BWOK

VNM

!!

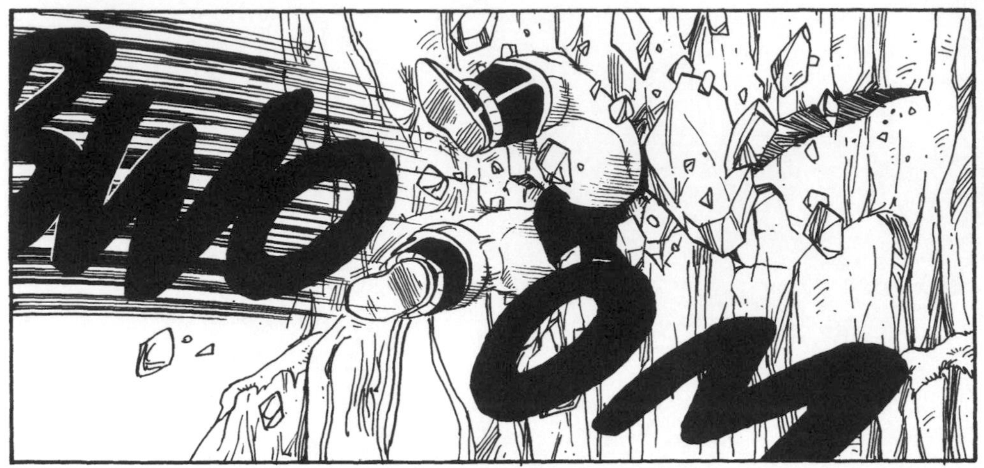

DZZ-------Z

HUHH
HUHH

GOMP...

VOON

!!

WHRRRR...
RRRR
TMP

NOW... !!!
I'VE HAD ENOUGH... !!!!

AH... AH... !
DIE !!!!

KRAK

!!
FWA

DOOO

DOOM

KRMBL
KRMBL...

HWOOO

HEH!!

?!

PI...
PICCOLO...?

G-GO... HAN...
...RUN...

GWRR....

DMMM
WH...
...WHY...?

...!

...WHY DID YOU SAVE ME...?

I TOLD YOU...TO RUN...
HU... HURRY...

DON'T DIE, PICCOLO! DADDY WILL COME SOON!
P- PLEASE... DON'T DIE!!

THOSE IDIOTS... MAKING US KILL THEM IN THE WRONG ORDER...
OH WELL... IT ALL ENDS UP THE SAME...

VWEE~···N

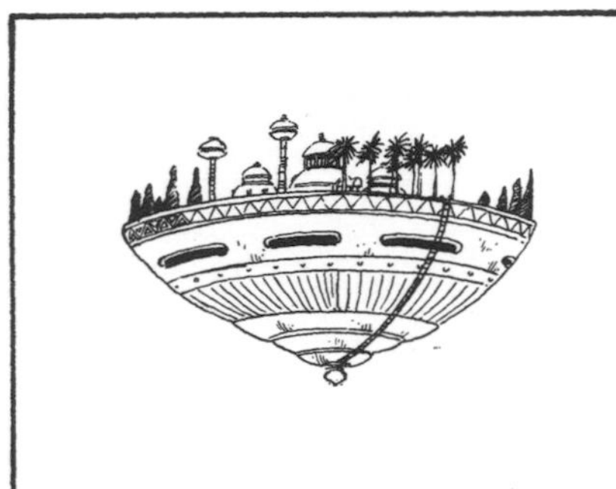

ONE OF THE CHI POWERS I FEEL IS GETTING SMALLER...
SOME-ONE'S DYING... !!

HUFF
HUFF

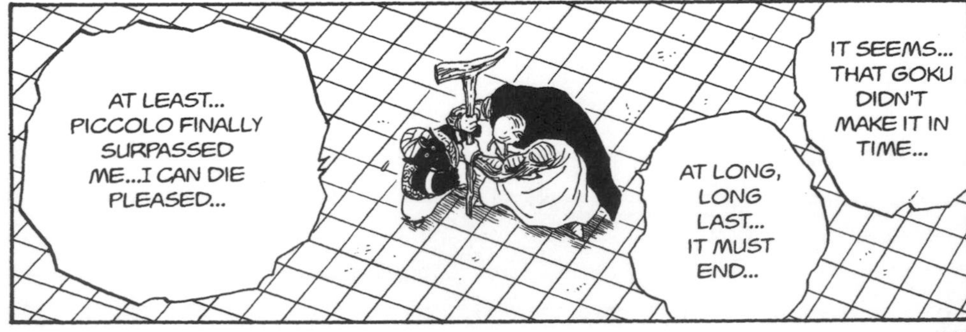

IT SEEMS... THAT GOKU DIDN'T MAKE IT IN TIME...
AT LONG, LONG LAST... IT MUST END...
AT LEAST... PICCOLO FINALLY SURPASSED ME...I CAN DIE PLEASED...

OH, THE SHAME... PICCOLO THE GREAT... THE INCOR-RUPTIBLE EVIL...
...SAVING A CHILD... HOW PATHETIC... HEH... HEH HEH...

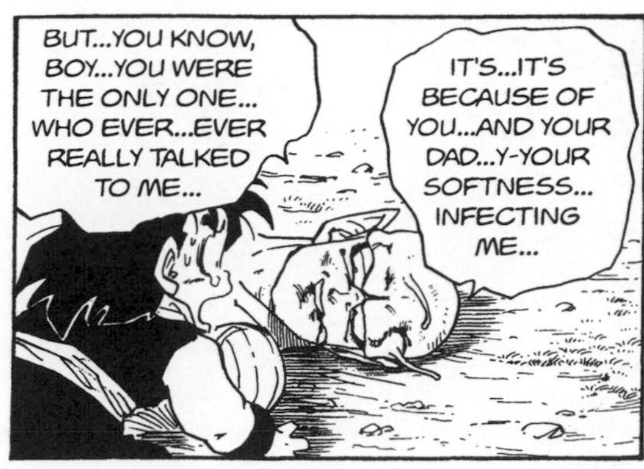
IT'S...IT'S BECAUSE OF YOU...AND YOUR DAD...Y-YOUR SOFTNESS... INFECTING ME...
BUT...YOU KNOW, BOY...YOU WERE THE ONLY ONE... WHO EVER...EVER REALLY TALKED TO ME...

THE COUPLE OF MONTHS... I SPENT WITH YOU...WEREN'T REALLY...SO BAD...

...GOHAN...
...DON'T... DIE...

BMM
!!

!!
I-IT'S GONE... !

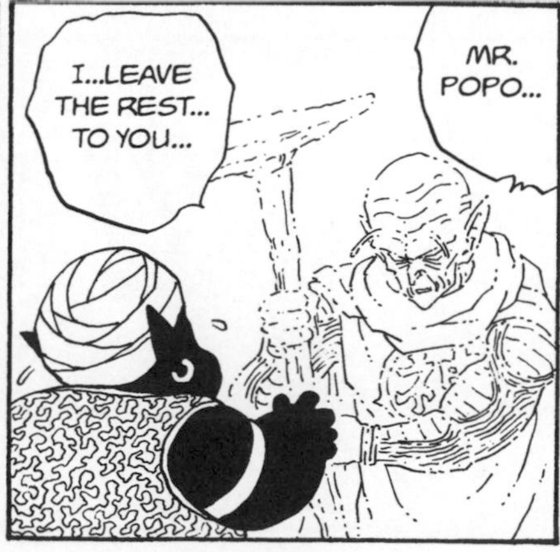
MR. POPO...
I...LEAVE THE REST... TO YOU...

FFF
K-KAMI-SAMA !!

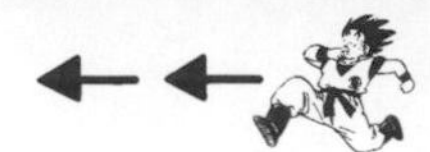

* THE "DEMON FLASH"—PICCOLO'S SIGNATURE MOVE!

TH-THAT POWER...!! IS THAT... GOHAN... ?!
BZZT BZZT
!!

POWER 2,800... !!
AS I THOUGHT! THEIR POWERS FLUCTUATE TREMEN-DOUSLY!!

2,800, EH... ?!!

RAAUGH!!!

BWAK

Z-BOOM

N-NOT BAD...
FOR A SHRIMP...
HEH... THAT ACTUALLY STUNG... A LITTLE BIT...

HIS POWER DROPPED ALL THE WAY DOWN...
IT SEEMS HE USED IT ALL UP JUST NOW...

TH-THEY'RE TOO STRONG... THEY'RE JUST TOO STRONG...

I'M SORRY, PICCOLO...
I...I COULDN'T BEAT 'EM FOR YOU...I C-CAN'T EVEN RUN AWAY ANYMORE...

SHK...
BMM

THIS CAN'T BE IT...!!
NO... !!

HAAH HA HA!! I CAN'T WAIT TO SEE KAKARROT'S FACE WHEN HE FINDS HIS SON CRUSHED TO A PULP!!

GWOM

!!

SHUMP

?!

EH
?!

...?!

FFFF
FWAA...

...K...
KI...
KINTO'UN...
?!

WH-
WHAT
IS
THAT...
?!

HSST

!!

SHHH...

Tp

G... GOKU... !!

WELL... FINALLY... !

DBZ:30 • The Quiet Wrath of Son Goku

GOKU... !
WE'VE WAITED SO LONG...!

D...
DADDY... !

WHAT DO YOU THINK YOU'RE DOING HERE, KAKARROT ?
NOT TO MAKE SOME RIDICULOUS SPEECH ABOUT "DEFEATING US," I HOPE?

EH
?!
SHK...

......

PICCOLO...

HE DIED... TRYING TO SAVE ME...
......

TENSHINHAN...

YAMCHA...

SNORT DON'T TELL ME YOU'RE SHOCKED TO FIND YOUR LAME FRIENDS DEAD! COME TO THINK OF IT, THERE WAS ANOTHER ONE...BLOWN TO PIECES...
WELL, NO NEED TO GRIEVE! YOU'LL SEE 'EM ALL SOON ENOUGH! AND RIGHT AFTER YOU CAME BACK TO LIFE, TOO!

CHAOZU TOO, HUH...?
HA HA...

AND KAMI-SAMA...

pi pi pi-
HIS POWER IS INCREASING STEADILY...

HEY!
WHAT IS IT, EH?! READY TO DIE ALREADY?!

WELL, HERE'S MY WAY OF SAYING HELLO !!

?!!
THIS WAY, GOHAN.

WH...
WHAT... ?!

...HE'S FAST... !

I'M SORRY I'M LATE... YOU DID WELL HOLDING OUT...
SPLIT THIS BETWEEN THE TWO OF YOU...
HUH... ?

A SENZU BEAN... M-MASTER KARIN STILL HAD THOSE... ?
IT'S THE LAST ONE.

N-NO...YOU SHOULD SAVE IT...JUST IN CASE! WE CAN'T DO MUCH TO HELP EVEN IF WE DO GET BETTER...
QUIT WORRYING. IF YOU'RE NOT GONNA EAT IT, I'M GONNA THROW IT AWAY!

THEN ***YOU*** SHOULD HAVE IT, GOKU!
I'M FINE, I ALREADY HAD ONE.
...RRG... !!

I-IN THAT CASE...
MNG MNG...

GOHAN... YOU TOO.
Snif...
OKAY...

SHP!
HEH... HEH HEH HEH!

YOU'VE IMPROVED A LOT, KURIRIN... I CAN FEEL IT...
I THOUGHT I HAD...I TRIED... BUT THEY WERE TOO STRONG...

I LET THEM ALL DIE...

AND GOHAN... YOU'VE CHANGED SO MUCH! YOU TRAINED WELL!

P... PICCOLO... TAUGHT ME...
B-BUT I COULDN'T DO ANY-THING...

PICCOLO DIED... WE CAN'T USE THE DRAGON BALLS ANY-MORE...NOBODY CAN COME BACK TO LIFE...
.....
.....

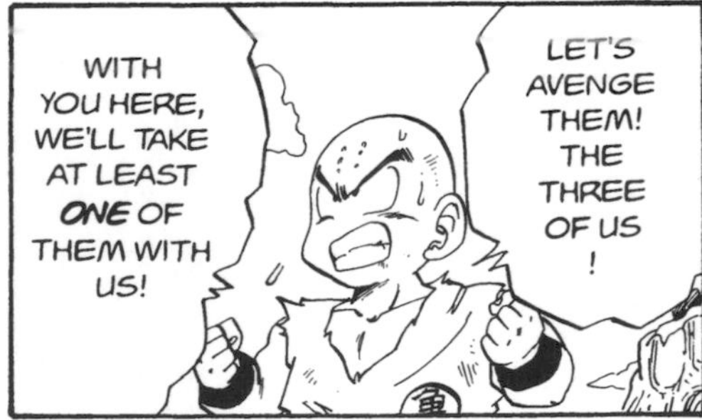
LET'S AVENGE THEM! THE THREE OF US!
WITH YOU HERE, WE'LL TAKE AT LEAST ***ONE*** OF THEM WITH US!

YOU TRAINED UNDER KAIŌ, RIGHT? THE LORD OF THE WORLDS?!
...YEAH.

BUT I'LL FIGHT THEM ALONE.
YOU TWO STAY CLEAR, SO YOU DON'T GET HURT.

ALONE... ?!

THAT'S INSANE!! EVEN FOR YOU!! THEIR POWER IS BEYOND IMAGINATION !!
H-HE'S RIGHT, DADDY... !!

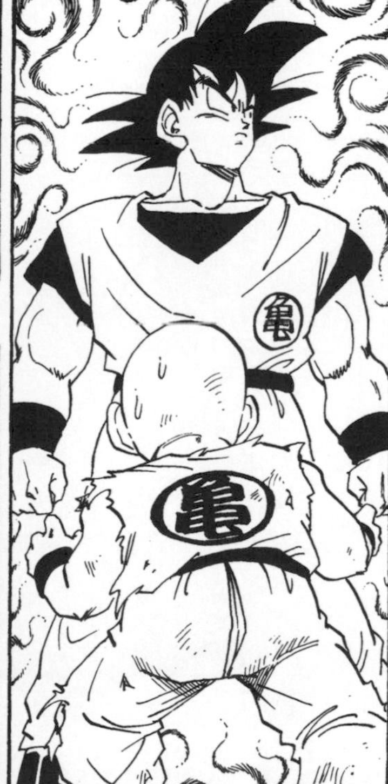

HRRR..
.....

W-WE BETTER DO AS HE SAYS...
AND LEAVE IT TO HIM...
B-BUT... !

HURRY!! *NOW!!*
D-DADDY... !!

I-I'VE NEVER SEEN GOKU... SO ANGRY.
THERE'S NO PLACE FOR US HERE...

WHAT'S THAT LOOK ON YOUR FACE...? I DON'T LIKE IT...
I WAS HOPING YOU WOULDN'T WANT TO DIE SO QUICKLY... *HEH HEH HEH...*

THERE'LL BE NO MERCY FOR YOU...
I'LL GIVE YOU WHAT YOU GAVE MY FRIENDS!

BBBMM...

POWER
7,000...
8,000...
!!

IT
CAN'T
BE...
!!!

UH...
?!

HRORR...

...!!

HSSS

HWOOOO---
V-VEGETA...
WHAT WAS KAKARROT'S POWER AGAIN?!

OVER... 8,000...
KRNCH

8,000... ?!
IT'S A MISTAKE! IT'S BROKEN!

DON'T WORRY.
I WON'T USE THE KAIŌ-KEN ON YOU YET...

YOU'LL NEVER BE A MATCH FOR ME!!

HWAA--!!

DOOM

WHAT ?!!

SHLAMM

HWA?

UNH... !!
HOW'D YOU GET... BEHIND ME... ?!

DBZ:31 • Vengeance

I...I'LL **DESTROY** YOU !!!

WHAT DID YOU SAY ?!!!!
WHAT... ?!!

YOU TALK A LOT. BUT YOU DON'T BACK IT UP.

STRANGE... HIS POWER IS COMPLETELY DIFFERENT FROM BEFORE!

H-HOW... HOW DID HE...DO THAT... ?

YOU'RE SAYING **I**... AM JUST ***TALK***...?!!!

I COULD TELL BY THAT BLOW.

HEH...HEH HEH...
YOU COULD TELL, HUH...?!

SO WHAT CAN YOU TELL... FROM ***THIS***?!

VOOOON

BA-
BA-
BA-
BAM

BABABABA

NH !!!!

D-DID YOU SEE THAT...?
UHH...

HOW DID KAKARROT GAIN SO MUCH POWER SO QUICKLY?

CHHHHH

AA !!!

PAM
NYAAAAA!!!

ZHMMM

GAAAR....!!!!

THAT WAS FOR CHAOZU !!!

TYAAA!!!
FFFN

BWOK
THAT WAS FOR YAMCHA !!!

DOKK
SKRRR
YOU... SCURRYING BRAT !!!!
DOOM

THIS ONE...
...I WON'T DODGE !!

HYAAAA!!!!

BOM

PIPI---
PIPIPI----

WH...
WHAT THE... ?!!

HE BLEW IT AWAY...WITH *CHI* ALONE... !!
SHAAH

THIS ONE'S FOR TENSHINHAN !!

SHWP

VNNNN

AND **THIS** IS FOR **PICCOLO** !!!

WOK

WRRRRRRR

GWMM

YOOOOU
...!!!!!
YOU
DARE...
?!!

WELL.
YOU'RE AS TOUGH AS I EXPECTED.

I AM AN ELITE WARRIOR OF THE NOBILITY!! I'LL HAVE NO LOWER-CLASS PUNK LIKE *YOU* PUSH ME AROUND!!!!

W-WOW!! GOKU'S... UNBELIEV-ABLE !!!
HE MIGHT ACTUALLY WIN THIS... !!!
G-GO, DADDY... !!!

NAPPA!!!! GET AHOLD OF YOURSELF, FOOL!!!!
HE CAN'T BEAT YOU IF YOU KEEP YOUR HEAD!!! CALM DOWN!!!!

...!!

Y-YOU'RE RIGHT...! THANKS, VEGETA...
I...I WASN'T THINKING...

IDIOT...! AT THIS RATE, I MAY HAVE TO FIGHT PERSONALLY.....

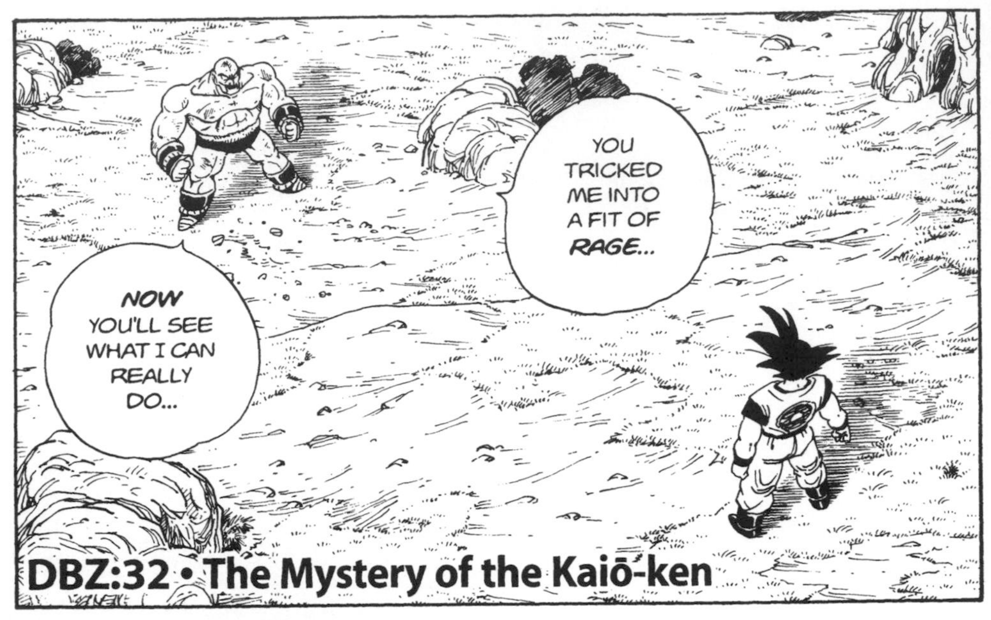

YOU TRICKED ME INTO A FIT OF RAGE...
NOW YOU'LL SEE WHAT I CAN REALLY DO...

DBZ:32 • The Mystery of the Kaiō-ken

ARE YOU READY...
...KAKARROT?

AH. THAT'S IT.
THIS IS WHAT I WANTED.

HEH. HE'S BLUFFING...

NO. HE HAS POWER TO SPARE...AND UTTER CONFIDENCE IN HIMSELF...

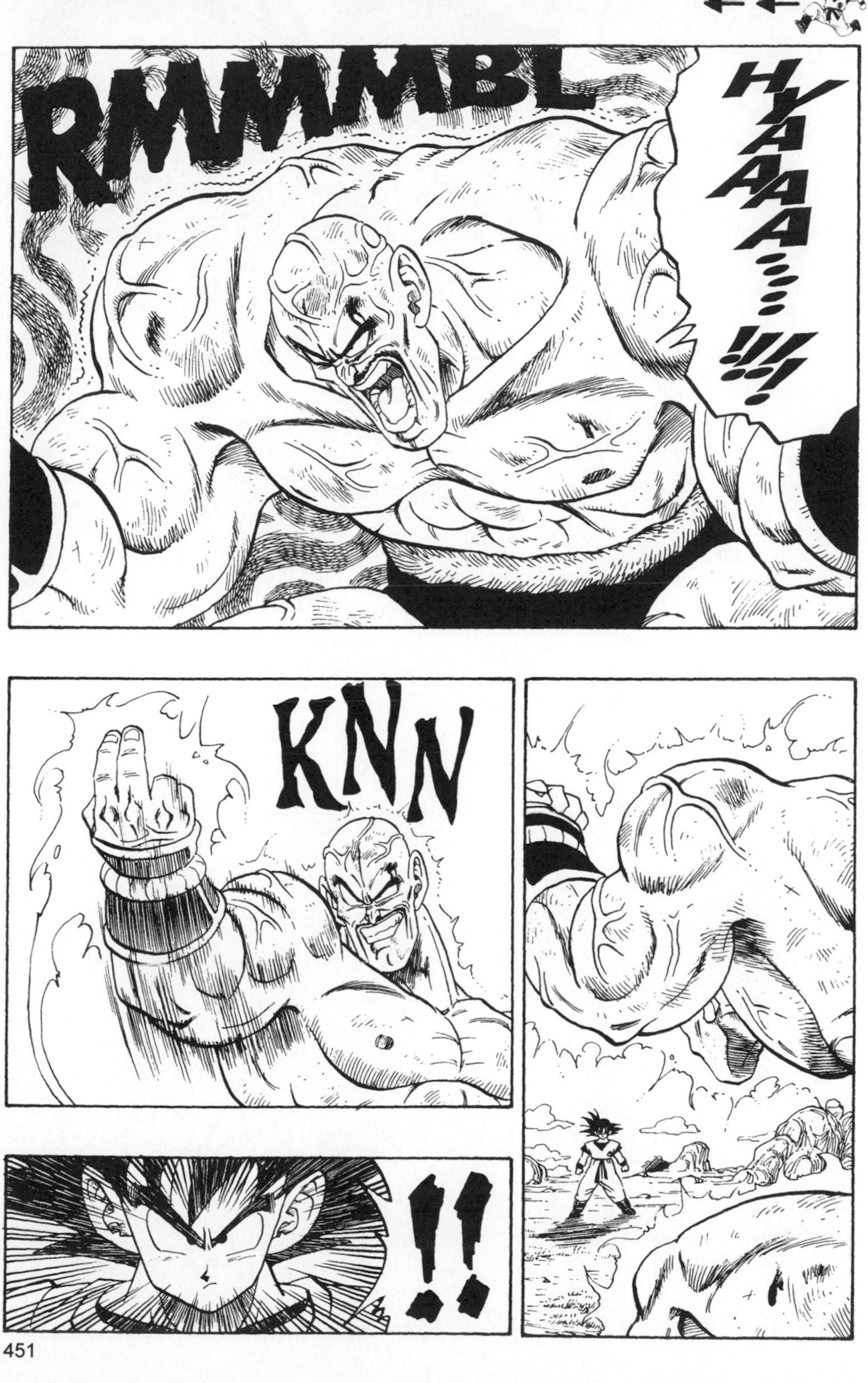

HYAAAA...!!!
RMMMBL

KNN

!!

SHWA

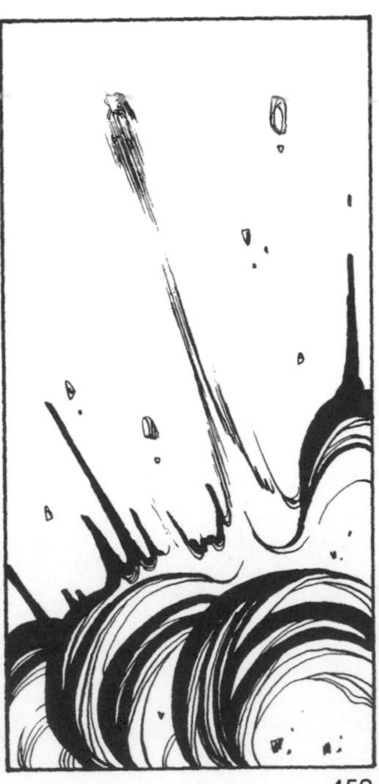

!!

VNN

SHH

K-
BA
BA
BA
BABABA

BA-BAM

YEAH!
THAT WAS MUCH BETTER!
HEH... BETTER, HUH?

I'LL MAKE SURE THAT'S THE LAST WISECRACK YOU EVER MAKE!
THIS IS IT, KAKARROT!

KP-PAA
?!

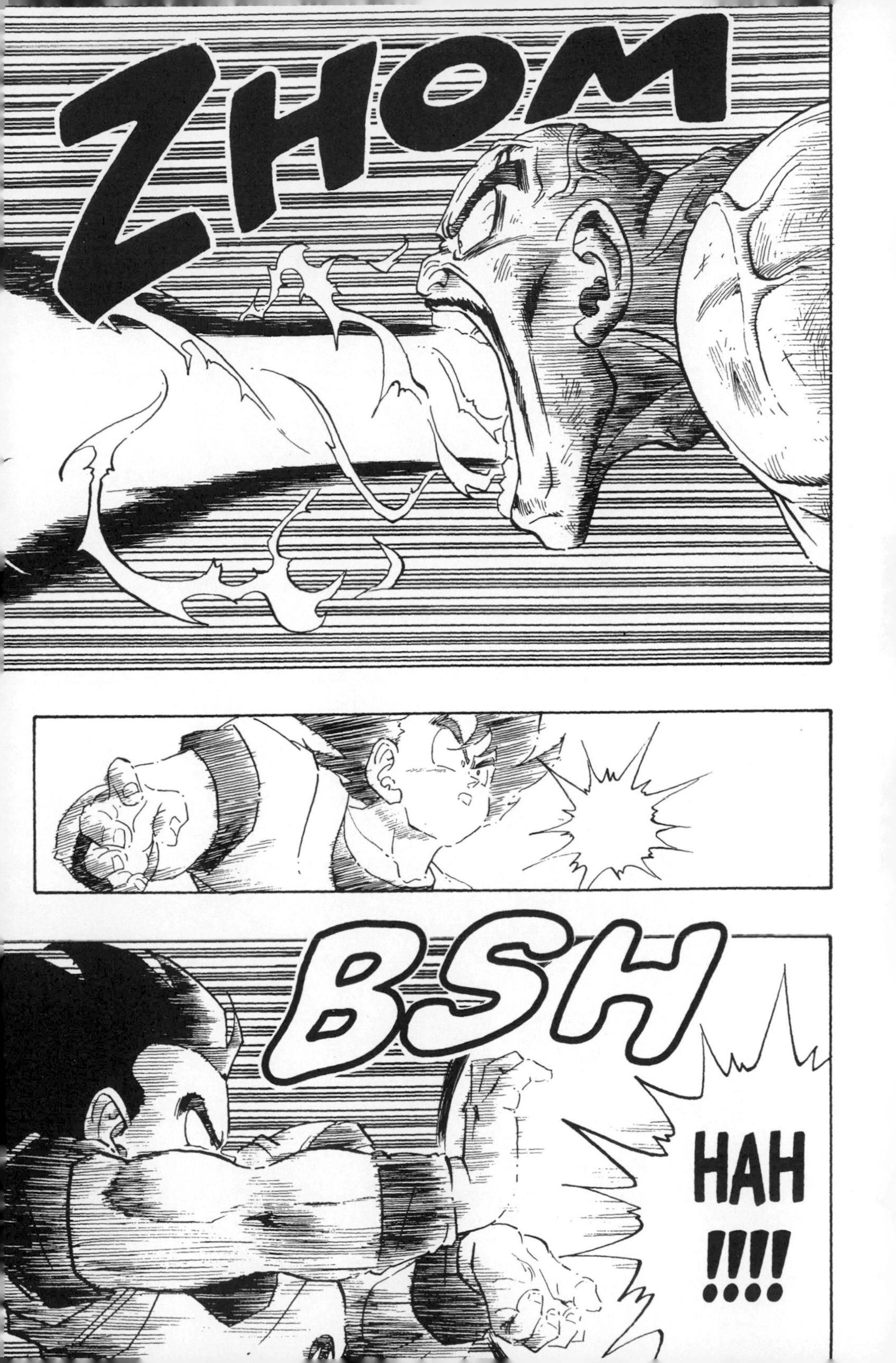

ZHOM

BSH
HAH
!!!!

SHBOOM
WAH !!!
FWAAA
TO DEFLECT IT...AT THAT DISTANCE!
UNBELIEVABLE... !!

PHEW
THAT ONE MADE ME SWEAT...!!

IT...IT CAN'T BE...!!! TH-THAT WAS MY...MY ULTIMATE TECHNIQUE... !!!
HE...HE JUST.... BOUNCED IT OFF... !!

HE REALLY *IS* TOUGH...! TOOK MY FIREBALL HEAD ON...!!
THIS COULD TAKE FOREVER...

THAT'S ENOUGH!! GET DOWN HERE, NAPPA!!! IT'LL TAKE FOREVER WITH YOU!
I'LL FINISH HIM *MYSELF* !!

..... !!

RIDICULOUS...
HAVING TO TROUBLE MYSELF AGAINST SOMETHING LIKE KAKARROT...

......

YEAH... FINALLY...
WE GET TO SEE THAT BIG JERK *AFRAID*.....

CURSE YOU... CURSE YOU TO HELL, BOY...
MAKING ME SURRENDER YOUR EXECUTION... TO VEGETA...

HEH

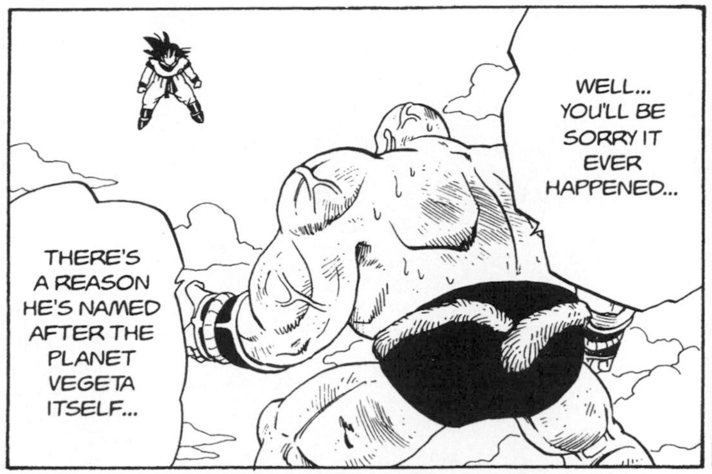
WELL... YOU'LL BE SORRY IT EVER HAPPENED...
THERE'S A REASON HE'S NAMED AFTER THE PLANET VEGETA ITSELF...

I'LL LEAVE YOU TO HIM BECAUSE HE ORDERED ME TO...
SHUUU--M
BUT I WON'T BE SATISFIED LEAVING THINGS AS THEY ARE...

?

HEH

?!

!!
GOHAN !!!!
KURIRIN... !!

!!

GYUUN

NO USE!!!!!

SHHHH

I'LL NEVER MAKE IT!!!!!

KP-PAA

KAIŌ-KEN!!!

PYOW

!!

KIIIN

GM

N......
G.....
H......
!!!
UH
?!

DN...SH

FWA

HE WON'T BE FIGHTING ANY-MORE...
TAKE HIM HOME... AND STAY THERE !!

AH...... AAHH...... !!!
V.... VEGETA...... !!!

WHAT... HAPPENED... ?
FOR AN INSTANT...HIS SPEED AND POWER MULTIPLIED !!

OOO~O

DBZ:33 • The Last of Nappa

N...NN...
IT...IT
HURTS...!

IMPOSSIBLE... NO ONE... JUST MULTIPLIES HIS POWER LIKE THAT...!!

GUH...GOKU... HOW'D YOU DO THAT...? WAS THAT... SOMETHING YOU WERE TAUGHT BY THE LORD OF WORLDS...?

YEAH...
IT'S CALLED KAIŌ-KEN !

YOU CONTROL ALL THE CHI IN YOUR BODY...AND AMPLIFY IT FOR A HEARTBEAT.
IF YOU GET IT RIGHT, YOUR POWER AND SPEED AND EVERYTHING SUDDENLY JUST GO ZOOM...

A... AMAZING !!
Y-YOU MEAN... YOU'RE EVEN STRONGER THAN YOURSELF...?!

IF ONLY I COULD HEAR WHAT THEY'RE SAYING...

WHAT'RE YOU MESSING AROUND FOR, THEN ?!
IF YOU HAD THAT UP YOUR SLEEVE, YOU SHOULDA JUST CUT LOOSE AT THE FIRST–

AHEM... SORRY... IT DOESN'T WORK THAT WAY...
IF I DON'T CONTROL MY CHI PERFECTLY WHILE I'M GOOSING IT UP...WELL, I CAN BEAT MYSELF...

HUH ?!

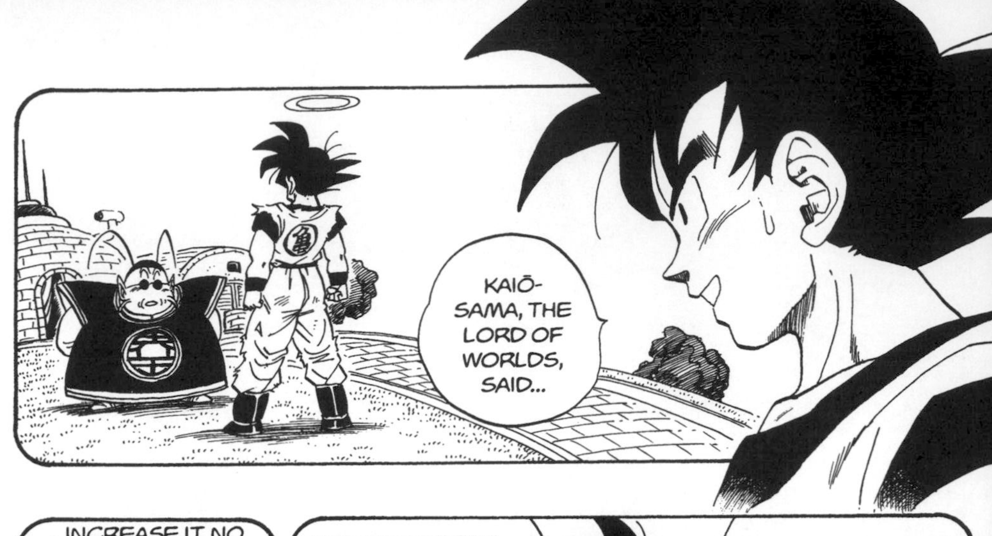
KAIŌ-SAMA, THE LORD OF WORLDS, SAID...

SON GOKU, YOU HAVE COME FURTHER WITH THE KAIŌ-KEN THAN EVEN I HAVE...
BUT REMEMBER THAT AT YOUR PRESENT LEVEL OF SKILL, YOU MUST BEWARE OF OVERUSING IT. THE SLIGHTEST ERROR IN YOUR CONTROL, AND YOU MIGHT DESTROY YOURSELF...
INCREASE IT NO HIGHER THAN TWICE YOUR NORMAL POWER...DO YOU UNDERSTAND?

ANY MORE THAN THAT, AND THE TOLL ON YOUR BODY MAY PROVE TOO GREAT...
IT WILL NOT BE ABLE TO CONTAIN YOUR SURGING POWER, AND YOUR OWN CHI WILL EXPLODE...
OKAY, OKAY, I GET IT !

...SO THERE WE ARE.
OH... GREAT...

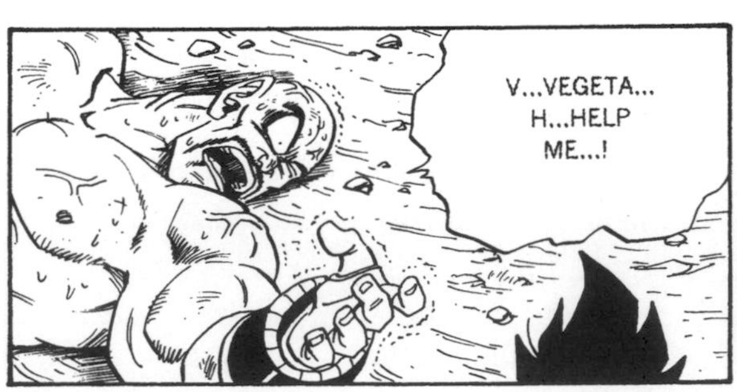
V...VEGETA... H...HELP ME...!

.....

GG

TH-
THANK YOU...
VEGETA...

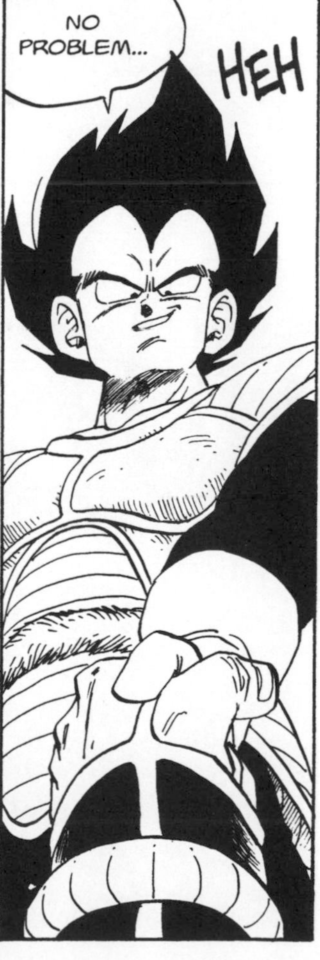
NO
PROBLEM...
HEH

GNNG

!!

!!

WHAT GOOD ARE YOU IF YOU CANNOT **FIGHT** ?!!

VU--UN

YAAA...A!!

WHAT ARE YOU DOING...?!! VEGETA!!

VEGEEEEEETA !!!

NONE
!!!!

WH-
WHAT
POWER...
!!!!!
KXX
KXX

N..
NO—
!!!!

ZHOOM

WSHHH

HWOOO----

bip

WHAT... KINDA... MONSTER IS HE?
H-HE'D KILL HIS OWN PARTNER...?

YOU'VE GOTTA GET BACK TO THE KAME HOUSE—NOW!
HUH ?!

.....
I... GET IT...

GOHAN! YOU HEARD HIM!!!
HUH?! B-BUT... BUT...

THE ENEMY'S TOO POWERFUL!! IF GOKU HAS TO WORRY ABOUT *US*, WE'LL ONLY BE GETTING IN THE WAY!!

SORRY...
HE'S EVEN STRONGER THAN I THOUGHT...

O-OKAY...
IF I HAVE TO...

DO ME A FAVOR, GOKU. FIGHT SOME-WHERE ELSE...!
WHAT?!
DO YOU WANT OUR FRIENDS' BODIES MANGLED WHEN THEY COME BACK TO LIFE...?

WHEN THEY COME BA-? BUT KURIRIN, PICCOLO'S DEAD, AND SO IS KAMI-SAMA...THE DRAGON BALLS ARE GONE FOREVER...
NOBODY'S EVER COMING BACK TO LIFE...

...!
KURIRIN... IS...IS THERE ANY WAY...?

IS THERE?!

I'LL EXPLAIN LATER...!
JUST TRUST ME...IF YOU *BEAT* HIM...!

IF I BEAT HIM...
YEAH...IT ALL COMES DOWN TO THAT, DOESN'T IT?
.....

WHAT'S KEEPING YOU, BOY ?!
FEELING A LITTLE SCARED, SUDDENLY ?!

ALL RIGHT... I'LL LEAD HIM SOME-WHERE ELSE...!
WISH ME LUCK, HUH?

GOKU...I'M SORRY WE HAVE TO LEAVE IT TO YOU ALONE...
YOU'D BETTER NOT DIE, OLD FRIEND !

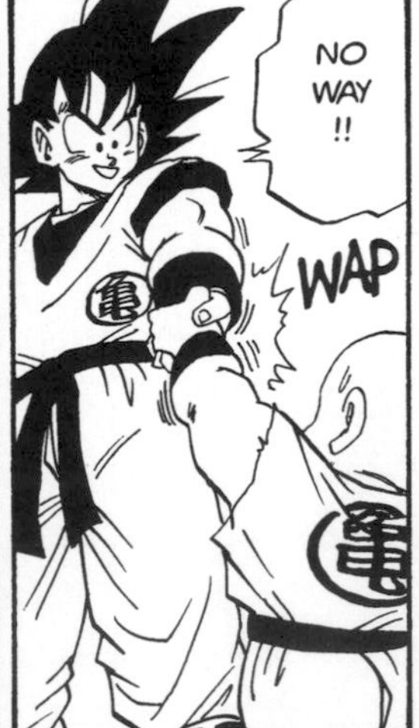
NO WAY !!
WAP

AFTER THIS IS DONE, SON... I'M TAKING YOU FISHING...!
YAY !!

SHHH

TM

YOU FIGURED OUT IT'S USELESS TO RUN... ?

WE'RE NOT FIGHTING HERE...

HAVE IT YOUR WAY.

BNN
BNN

......
DADDY...

VOOOO...N

HE'S KEEPING UP WITH ME WITH NO SWEAT... !

HYNN
HYNN

HERE !!
NOTHING LIVES IN THIS DESERT !

SHH
SHH

TM

TM

WHICH MAKES IT A FITTING PLACE TO DIE...
HEH HEH HEH...

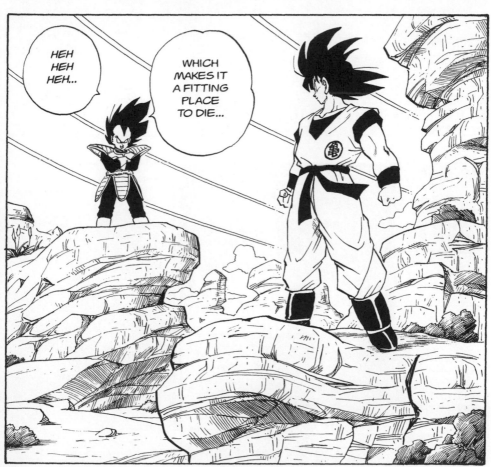

YOU SHOULD BE HONORED, YOU KNOW... A BOTTOM-TIER BOY LIKE YOU HARDLY EVER GETS A CHANCE TO PLAY WITH AN ELITE WARRIOR LIKE ME...

DBZ:34 • Mano a Maniac!!

WE SAIYANS ARE TESTED FOR COMBAT APTITUDE SOON AFTER WE'RE BORN...
THE PITIFUL BABES WITH LOW BATTLE-NUMBERS ARE SHIPPED OFF TO A PLANET WITH NO SERIOUS OPPONENTS...
JUST LIKE YOU WERE...

IF THAT'S HOW I GOT TO EARTH... I'M GRATEFUL.
ON THIS PLANET, WE KNOW THAT EVEN THE LOWEST-BORN CAN OUTDO THE ELITE IF THEY WORK HARD ENOUGH.

HEH... AT LEAST THEY HAVE A SENSE OF HUMOR...
NOW I'LL SHOW YOU THE WALL THAT YOU CAN NEVER SCALE WITH "HARD WORK" ALONE...

S...

Z...

HWOOOO...

VN

BBBMM

PP PAA
BBMM

HSS H

BNG
BBNNG

KMM

HW

WACH

?!

SHHH

HSSH

GNG

THIS ISN'T HOW YOU DEFEATED NAPPA!!

SHOW ME !!!!!!
WOKK

SKRRRRRR

TMM

TM

UNBELIEVABLE...
HE'S JUST JOKING AROUND.... AND HE'S STILL STRONGER AND FASTER THAN ME...

OKAY, THEN!
I'LL SHOW YOU.

BHOO---M

← ←

VNN
TYAH
!!!!!!

HSSST

SHPNG

!!
BOOOM

VOON
!!

BWOOM

TKKKK

KRAK

ZHOW
VNN
NK
WRR
!!

HEH...
IF THAT WAS YOUR BEST, I'M DISAP-POINTED...

...!

UNH !!!!

I CAN'T BELIEVE HIM...! BUT...IN A WEIRD WAY... I'M STARTING TO GET KIND OF EXCITED...!

TITLE PAGE GALLERY

Following are the title pages for the individual chapters as they appeared during their original serialization in *Weekly Shonen Jump* magazine in Japan from 1988 to 1995.

Five Years Later, A New Shadow Is Cast

DBZ:01 • The Mysterious Warrior from Space

DRAGON BALL

DBZ:02
Kakarrot

DBZ:03 • Tails of Future Not-Quite-Past

Hi, I'm Son
Gohan!
I'm 4 years old.
When I grow up,
I want to be a
great scholar.

SOMETHING SAIYAN THIS WAY COMES!

DBZ:04 · An Enemy in Common

AKIRA TORIYAMA
鳥山明
BIRD STUDIO

DBZ:05
An Unexpected Strength

DRAGON BALL
DBZ:06
Nothing Up My Sleeve...
23

DBZ:07 • Piccolo's Farewell to Arms?!

Can They Pull It Off?!

Akira Toriyama
鳥山明
BIRD STUDIO

DRAGON BALL
DBZ:08
A Surprise Appearance

DRAGON BALL

ドラゴンボール

DBZ:09 • Goku's Last Chance...

DRAGON BALL

ドラゴンボール

DBZ:10 • Sayonara, Goku

Dragonball

ドラゴンボール

...and then I died...

DBZ:11

A Warrior in Hell

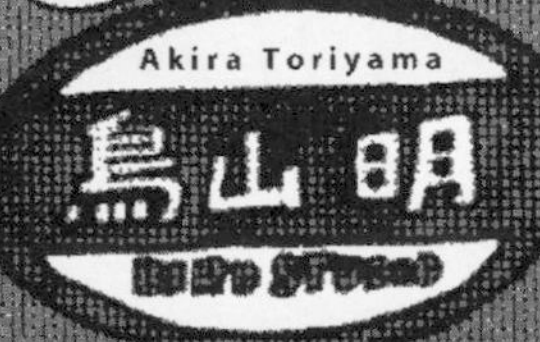

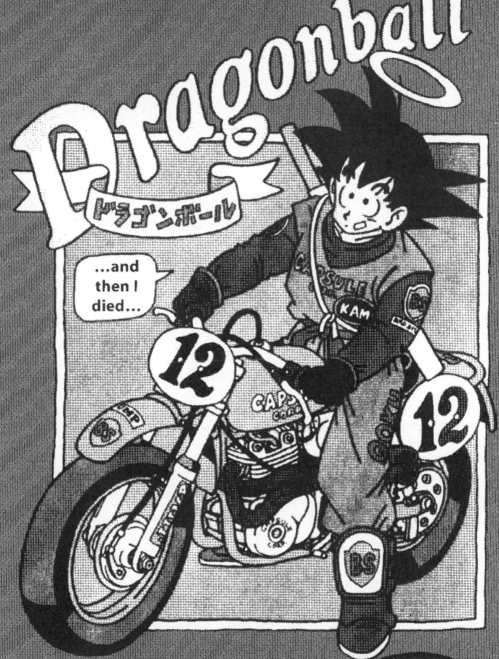

DRAGONBALL

DBZ:12 · Gohan and Piccolo

ドラゴンボール
DRAGON BALL
DBZ:13
Son Gohan, the Inconsolable

DRAGON

ドラゴンボール

DBZ:14 • Deeds Done by the Full Moon

DBZ:15
Goku and Gohan's Training Begins!!

DRAGON BALL
ドラゴンボール
DBZ:16
Masters and Students
KAMEHOUSE
CAPSULE CORPORATION
CAPSULE
64
BIRD STUDIO
920
51B07

DBZ:17 • The Hardest Time of His Death

DRAGON BALL

ドラゴンボール

DBZ:18
Closer... Closer...

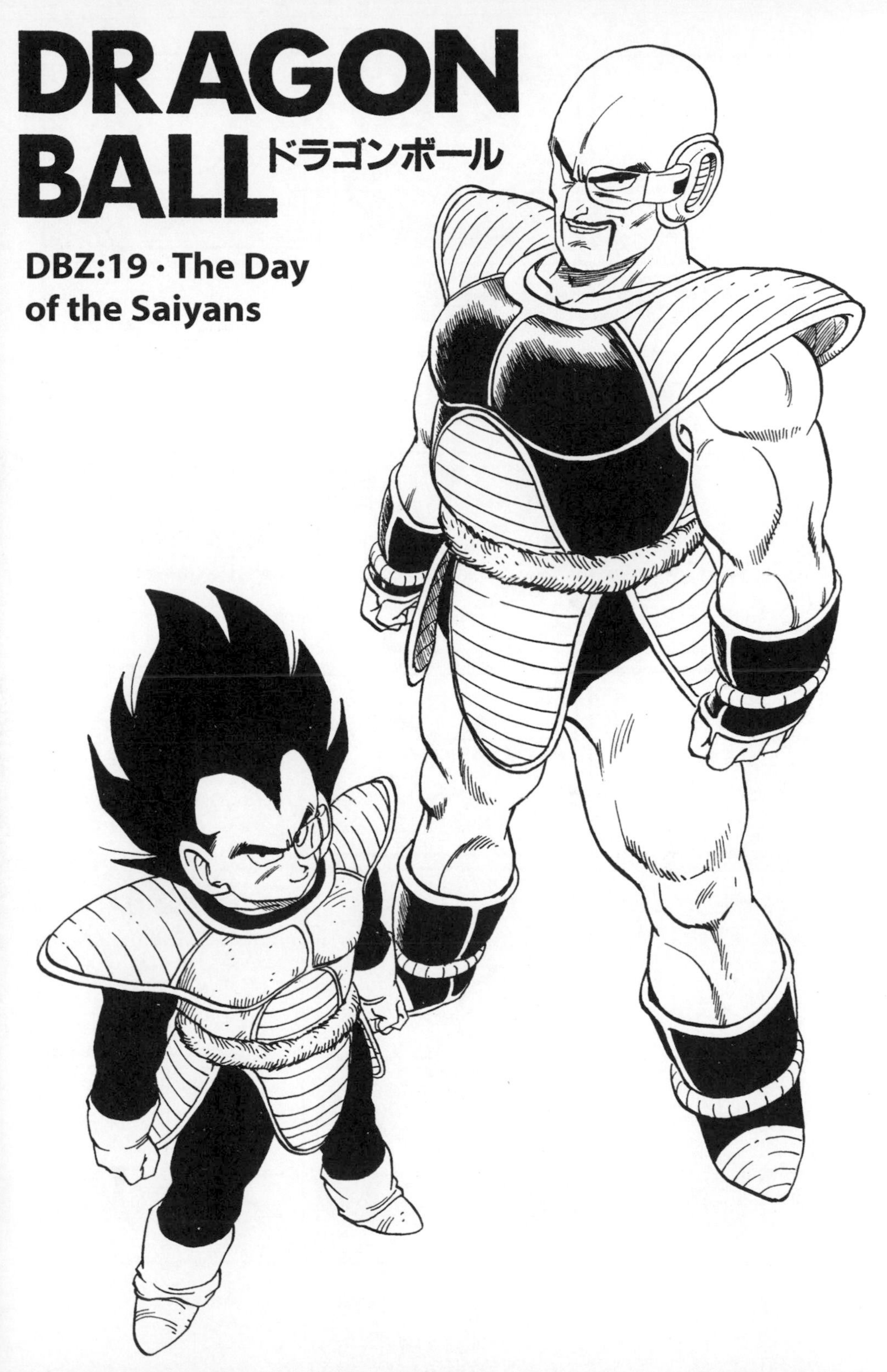
DRAGON BALL
ドラゴンボール
DBZ:19 · The Day of the Saiyans

DRAGON BALL

ドラゴンボール

DBZ:20 Let the Games Begin!

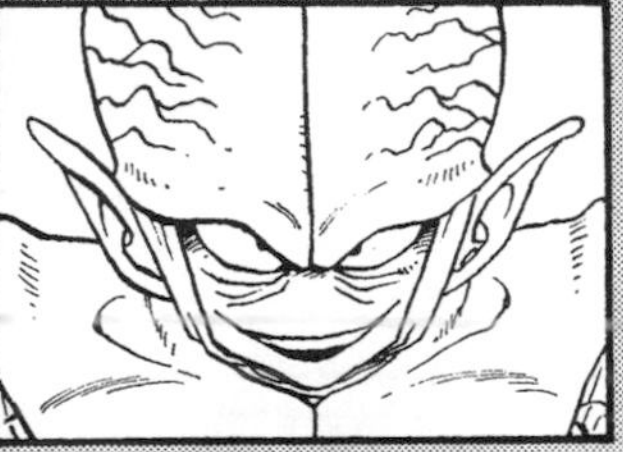

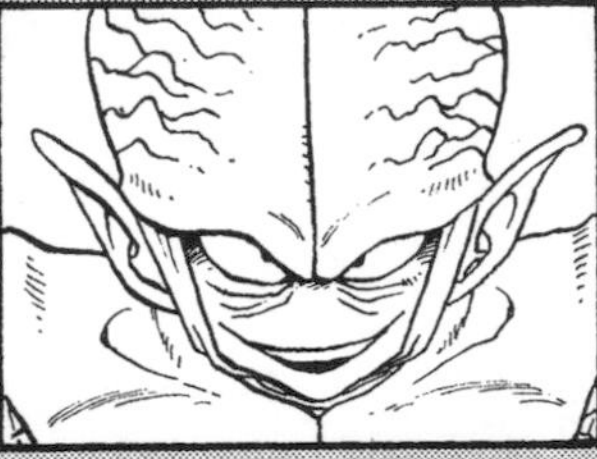

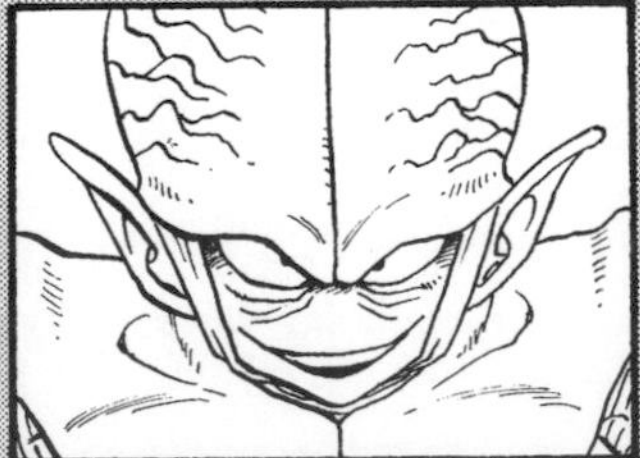

DBZ:21 • One Down...

Your Turn, Yamcha…
Show 'Em What Earthlings Can Do!

DBZ:22 • Heroes in Terror

DRAGON BALL

ドラゴンボール

DBZ:23 • Hope Runs Out

DRAGONBALL

DBZ:24

The Last Blast

DBZ:25 • Goku, Hurry!

Do Whatever You Have to, But Get Here Soon!!!

DBZ:26 • Back from the Other Side

DBZ:27 · The Time Draws Near...

DBZ:28 • The Death of a God!!

I'VE GOTTA MAKE IT IN TIME!!!

DRAGON BALL

ドラゴンボール

DBZ:29 • Piccolo's Last Stand

DBZ:30 • The Quiet Wrath of Son Goku

FOR DEPARTED FRIENDS…
A FORMER ENEMY…
AN HONORED TEACHER…
GOKU'S ANGER IS
RISING!!!

DRAGON BALL

ドラゴンボール

DBZ:31 · Vengeance

ドラゴンボール

DRAGON BALL

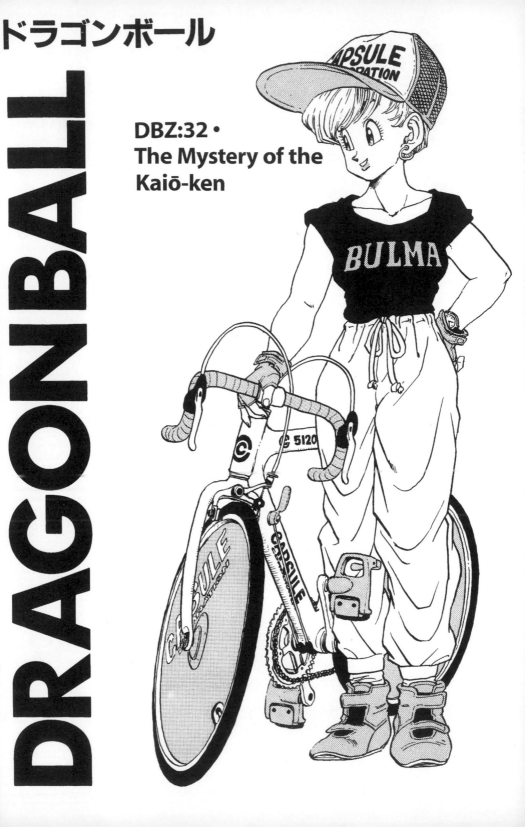

DBZ:32 • The Mystery of the Kaiō-ken

DBZ:33 · The Last of Nappa

DBZ:34
Mano a Maniac!!

AUTHOR NOTES

1989

VOLUME 1

Most of the time, when my assistants aren't around, I work in a TV room while sitting at the *kotatsu* [a low table]. Part of the reason is that I just can't get comfortable sitting in a chair at a desk. Also, it's kind of lonely working without the TV or a video on. But it's important not to get distracted by the TV and stop drawing. While I'm working, I always try to act like I'm not paying any attention to it. I'm such a good boy!

VOLUME 2

I don't know how many times I've said it—I hate the cold and I hate winter! I wish I could go skiing, but there's no way I would go. Why would I go out of my way to go someplace that's so cold? But on the other hand, I love it when it's hot, in the summertime! I get so excited! That's why it's mostly summer in my manga. I love the summer! Now if only there weren't any mosquitoes...

1989

1989

VOLUME 3

I, just like probably all of you, love Disneyland. (Though I've only been there six times...) It's because everything is done so professionally, down to the smallest details. Now that I think about it, I first got interested in drawing when I was in nursery school and I went to see *101 Dalmatians* at the movie theater. I was inspired by the great artwork. I am very grateful.

IN THE NEXT VOLUME

With the mighty Kaiō-ken amplifying his strength, Goku fights Vegeta in a desperate battle to save the world. But alone, Goku's new techniques may not be enough to defeat Vegeta's elite Saiyan powers. It looks like the last worn-out survivors of the conflict—Gohan, Kuririn, and Yajirobe—must rush back into the fray!

AVAILABLE NOW